Running Your Own Business

PERSONAL FINANCE GUIDES

In the same series:

Don't Pay Too Much Tax If You're Self–Employed

David Williams

Running Your Own Business

David Williams

THIRD EDITION

NICHOLAS BREALEY
PUBLISHING

L O N D O N

First published in Great Britain by
Nicholas Brealey Publishing Limited in 1994
21 Bloomsbury Way
London WC1A 2TH

ISBN   1-85788-092-7

British Library Cataloguing-in-Publication Data
A catalogue record for this book is available from the British Library.

Every care has been taken in preparing this book.The guidance it contains is sound at the time of publication but is not intended to be a substitute for skilled professional assistance except in the most straightforward situations. Because of this the author, the publishers and Allied Dunbar Assurance plc (or any other company within the Allied Dunbar Group) can take no responsibility for the outcome of action taken or not taken as a result of this book.

The views and opinions of Allied Dunbar may not necessarily coincide with some of the views and opinions expressed in this book which are solely those of the author and no endorsement of them by Allied Dunbar should be inferred.

The material herein which is Crown Copyright is reproduced with the permission of the Controller of Her Majesty's Stationery Office.

Typeset by Frere Publishing Services, 2 Whitehorse Street, London W1
Printed and bound in Great Britain by Biddles Ltd

Contents

Introduction

HUGE CHANGES have been taking place in our country over the last few years. We have stopped being a manufacturing country. Instead we are, above all, a service economy. Where once a million people worked in or near the mines, now only a few thousand are employed. It is, more than ever, important that those of us with the initiative and ideas to run our own businesses seize the moment. But it is not easy.

Where do you start? What are the chief problems? How much money is needed? When is it needed most? Do we need to set up a company? How do we work together? Is the idea for a new product a good one? What should be the approach to publicity? These, and many other questions, have to be considered if you are going to plan towards success.

This book tries to ensure you ask the right questions, and that you ask those questions of the right people. Some the book can answer, and does. But some of the most important questions are those you must ask yourself.

When you have worked through the book you will have been asked lots of questions. If you think through all the issues, and seek help where it is suggested, your business should be off to a strong start. Good luck!

Just as I have asked you to do, so in writing and updating this book I have made enquiries, taken advice and sought help from many people. Not least this has included friends, neighbours and family who had their brains picked or who have shared their own experiences. For this new edition, my thanks go to commentators and reviewers of past editions and particularly to David Vessey, Nick Brealey, Rupert Scott and my secretary Sandra Baird for help in preparing the new work. More generally, I must again acknowledge what I urge you to gain, support from the family, especially Lis, Edward, Tom and Richard.

David Williams

May 1994

1   *Getting started*

*T*HAT'S EASY. You already have. If not before, you started when you opened this book.

Like everyone else running or intending to run their own business, you have lots of questions needing answers before you really get going. There will be still more questions later. That's the reason for this book. It helps you ask the right questions, and helps you set about getting the right answers. It helps you think about the problems confronting your business. Read the book through quickly while thinking generally. Then come back to the areas on which you need or wish to spend more time when making your plans more definite. It will also help you set about getting advice from the right experts.

To help you work through your questions, and the answers to them, you need a pencil and some paper. So, before we go any further, find yourself a suitable sharp pencil, some sheets of paper or a notebook and, if you wish, an eraser too. Only when you have them should you turn the page.

You've found the pencil! Good. You'll need it to plan your business properly.

THE AIMS OF THIS BOOK

The first aim is to encourage you to look at yourself and assess why you want to run your own business (section 2). It then answers questions about how you start a business and the forms the business might take. Next, it aims to help you think through and plan all the important aspects of your business – the five Ps: Purpose, Product, Potential, People, Pounds. The importance of this plan is emphasised later in the book. The next part discusses the pounds, that is, the finance required to run your business and the accounts needed to control the cash. Then we look at what else is involved: products and how to market them, location, legal issues, and how to employ others. Finally, we look at the next stage, expansion. Why not have a quick look through before you get going, so you can see what's ahead. There is a useful list of addresses at the end.

The book tells you what planning and research you must do, and the decisions you must take. It also tells you when to get the experts in, and how to get the best from the free and subsidised advisory services available in most areas.

AND FOR THOSE WHO DIDN'T GET A PENCIL...

... ask yourself why. A management school sets all its candidates for entry a written examination. Candidates are told to turn up to the exam room armed with two sharp 2B pencils, an eraser and a ruler - and nothing else. As they enter the exam room, candidates are asked to show their equipment. Anyone who does not have exactly the equipment they were asked to bring is not allowed in to the exam room. They are excluded from, and have therefore failed, the exam. Why?

There is one brutal little lesson they have learned. The exam began long before they thought it did. They expected the questions to start when the three-hour session started. But no one else told them that. They had jumped to the wrong conclusion and had only themselves to blame for not taking notice of the advice and instructions.

Bearing in mind your business has also started, a pencil would be a very good idea. Keep it by you and write notes as you go along. Now, on to the next page and we'll really get down to business.

2   *Starting on your own*

L ET'S BEGIN at the beginning. There is one thing in common - or rather a whole series of things in common - to all your plans whatever you choose to do. It's **you**, and your strengths and weaknesses. It's with you we must start. People go into business for a wide variety of different reasons. Some make the move out of complete choice; others feel they have no other choice. A recent survey showed that many potential self-employed were staff who wanted to break out on their own for a variety of reasons. What are your reasons?

YOU'VE GOT A GOOD IDEA?

Many employees, while busy working for their employers, realise they could be doing the same thing better and more profitably for themselves. Or perhaps they could be running the business better than their employer. There have been many successful examples of management buy-outs in recent years. Even on a small scale it can work well. If you really do know your job, you may see a niche in the market and customers for a new product or service. If so, you may be in a strong position. But think it through thoroughly before you jump.

Self-employment is easily forgotten when people are leaving school or college. It's quite easy for prestigious bodies like the armed forces, wealthy businesses like banks, or glamour industries like airlines to mount impressive displays at local careers conventions. Putting up an attractive display for 'the self–employed' is not so easy, because it covers so many different things. Our society has been used over many years to others supplying our job opportunities for us, perhaps too used to it. This is not so of some of our minority communities. Their backgrounds make them more ready to set up their own businesses. Choice of career is partly an attitude of mind, and the more open it is the better.

Both help and advice are available especially for the young as we shall see later. And there are ways you can explore this choice of career just as thoroughly as any other. You'd be wrong to dismiss it as an option if you're the right kind of person.

CHOOSING YOUR CAREER?

In recent years many people have experienced the nasty shock of redundancy. Often it was through no fault of their own. They were, they thought, safely employed in a secure job. Then they learned one day that very few jobs are really secure, and theirs wasn't one of them. All too soon, they were unemployed. Perhaps there was some redundancy money, perhaps not. There are several schemes, and financial help, for you if this is what has happened to you.

Over the last few years, literally millions of people have found themselves redundant. Some have found other employment but many have not. Some have used the chance to make good again on their own, sometimes with the active

REDUNDANT?

help of their former employer. In the last few years there has been a marked increase in help for all self-employed people, and for this group in particular. Help and advice is available, especially at the beginning. This book explains where.

FED UP WITH YOUR JOB?

Many other people still in work are thoroughly fed up with what they are now doing. Though they didn't at first realise, their life was like being on a conveyor belt or production line. They are put on the conveyor belt by their parents. At the age of five they were off to school. This shunted them on for the next ten years or so. Then they were off to college or to a job suggested to them. Or they followed where their friends went, or perhaps they went to the only employer with jobs at the time.

One day the conveyor belt stops. Suddenly they realise that they want to run their own lives. But the experience is a new one to them, and they want to know what to do next. If that describes you, then you are right to be reading this book because before you do anything else, you need to think, and then plan. I have seen too many people decide one day they can't stand their job any longer, and just walk out.   Only afterwards they discover that their employer is quite happy to see them go. Their pay stops suddenly.

But the Social Security Office isn't so happy, and they get hardly any state benefit. Before long they're almost completely out of money. Their friends find it very puzzling, and the family start grumbling. They have no idea what to do next. No one else seems interested. Make sure you always think about what to do next.

Perhaps you are looking for the challenge of living on your wits. You want to avoid the constraints of others asking what you are doing, and demanding your explanations for what is, or should be, happening. Your wish may be to be independent, not just of being told what to do, but of other people's way of thinking about things and doing things. You want the satisfaction of getting it right yourself.

These are just some reasons why people become self-employed. With over ten per cent of the working population now regarded as self-employed, there are likely to be many others. Your reasons may be totally different to all those above. Maybe there is a mixture of reasons. What are <u>your</u> reasons?

Get your pencil, and write out your answers to these two questions:

I want to run my own business because:

....
....
....
....
....
....
....
....
....
....
....
....
....
....
....
....
....
....
....

<u>WANT TO BE YOUR OWN BOSS?</u>

I think I will be good at it because:

....
....
....
....
....
....
....
....
....
....
....

Were you expecting the second question? Are you happy with the answer you have given to the question? Is it a good answer? Perhaps those are unfair questions. What does being 'good' at running a business involve? That is, of course, what much of this book is about and we're only on page 16 at the moment!

The question is a crucial one because not everyone is the right sort of person to be self-employed. Some are 'naturals' at it, while many others can get there with hard work. One thing is for sure. You need, in the words of the oracle, to 'know thyself' before you start. You can fool me with the answers you give - but don't fool yourself. Let's look at the strengths and weaknesses you possess.

WHAT WAS YOUR LAST JOB?

The best place to start is your present job or area of study, or what you were last doing when at work. What were the good and bad sides of that work? In particular, if you are thinking of giving up a job, what is it about the job that you can't stick? Is it a personality clash with the boss or your fellow staff? If so, is it their fault or yours? If it's your fault, how will becoming self-employed help? In what ways were you good at that job, and what parts did you find difficult? Much as you would like to start from somewhere else, you can't.

Those are all questions designed to make you think about the real you. That is because it's you that you're going to have to work with all the time in your new business. As a help, I've set out a list of questions and points below. Think about each point carefully. It may help to write notes beside each question as you go along. And remember, be honest. You owe it to yourself.

WHAT ARE YOUR STRENGTHS?

Personality

How tough are you? If the going gets rough will you stick it out? Did you, last time you hit a problem?

Are you a self-starter? Do you motivate yourself, or do you need others to give you the ideas or example?

Are you prepared to take decisions, especially hard ones? And not blame others if you get it wrong?

Did you take responsibility, last time you made a mistake, or is it always someone else's fault?

Are you good at organising yourself or other people?

Health

How good are you at coping with stress and strain?

Can you work long hours without collapsing in a heap?

Can you survive without holidays, and losing your weekends, if the business needs your time?

How many times have you been ill in the last few years? Are those problems going to recur?

What would your doctor say about you taking on your own business?

Should you ask him or her?

Dealing with other people

How well do you get on with other people socially? Do you have many friends and contacts?

How well do you get on with others at work? Are you a good leader at work, on the sports field, at the local youth club, anywhere?

Are you good at taking advice from others?

Are you the sort of person people rely on, or do you tend to rely on others?

Self-confidence

Do you believe in yourself, and have confidence in your own abilities and decisions?

Experience

What training and qualifications do you have for the business you want to run?

What work experience do you have of that kind of business?

Are you experienced in managing your own time and money, or that of other people?

THE RIGHT ANSWERS?

There is no one right answer to all these questions. However, if you cannot say 'yes' to the question about believing in yourself then you really do need to think very hard before you go any further. After all, if you do not have confidence in your own abilities, how can anyone else be expected to take you seriously? You can tell, can't you, within a minute of meeting people for the first time whether they are self-confident. Equally, other people will judge you just as quickly, and just as firmly.

Your state of health will matter more for some jobs than others. Indeed some people fighting serious disabilities find one way of doing it is through self-employment in an appropriate area of work. If that applies to you, you can get special help from several sources (see the section on outside help).

Particular demands of different businesses mean that the same answers are not needed to all the questions. But people who are best at self-employment are people possessing more than the average of some special qualities. They need:

Lots of energy and confidence

A more than average amount of self-reliance and

A clear awareness of their own strengths and weaknesses.

Above all, they need the **'bounce back factor'**, a mixture of energy, confidence, will power, persistence, self-reliance, even courage. It is the ability to take knocks and blows and not give up - still to be in the action when others have retired from it. How far do you have those abilities?

Although most people think they know themselves well, they are not always the best people to answer questions about themselves. Their immediate family and close friends often know how they will behave as well as, and sometimes better than, they do. What do your family and your friends think of your ideas?

Getting your family behind what you are doing is particularly important. Research shows that those who start their own businesses with their family behind them are more likely to succeed. Success can be as much as four times as likely as for those whose families do not support them. Even better, as we shall discuss later, if the family are prepared to help do the work.

If you are a family man or woman you owe it to your family to take their views fully into account. It is their livelihood and, often, home which is at risk as well as yours. And if they are on your side, they can be tremendous allies. Perhaps your wife or husband ought to be your partner in your new business, and not just a supporter or part-time employee.

Similarly, your friends can be of enormous value. Again, maybe the business would be better run by two or more partners, even if some are only part-time. They can help you find customers and ideas. Or they can tell you that they think the idea is wrong (but often won't, unless you ask them to be absolutely honest).

What does all this self-questioning tell you? I do not know. You do. If you have that 'bounce back factor' and your family and friends are right behind you, then we need to take your plans very seriously. But if what all this tells you is that your dream ought to remain just that, then you have not wasted your time. You know your future should lie elsewhere. If in spite of that information, you still go ahead, you may be making a serious mistake. Now is the time to redesign your plans and start on a firmer base.

If you think I'm being very negative, you are absolutely right! Why? I'm not trying to put you off becoming self-employed if you know what you are doing. I am trying, rather, to make sure you stop and think before you commit yourself, because many before you have not done so.

Every year a considerable number of small businesses fail completely and cease business. A much greater number - well over half - will fail to provide the high levels of material wealth some seek in their own business. By no means all of those are failures. Some stay small because that is what the people running them want. Their objectives are different. Perhaps yours are too. How did you answer the questions at the beginning of this section? Other businesses were meant to be bigger but did not make it. In some of these cases it is for the most basic reason: the person running the business was not up to it. Two other basic reasons are a failure to plan and a failure to take proper advice. You have been warned!

WHAT KIND OF BUSINESS?

You probably have some idea of the kind of business you aim to pursue. Even so, you still need to think very hard about how you are going to use your skills, inventions or ideas in your business. If you are not already tied to exploiting a particular line of business, your choice should be a matter of careful thought. Try to identify areas of activity that make the fullest use of your skills, abilities and material resources. That way you start as far along the road to success as you can.

If you are short of ideas or want to check them out, you can start right in your own home with the Yellow Pages phone book. Look for all the different kinds of business there are. Then note how many other people are already exploiting your idea in your locality. Between Abattoirs and Zoos in my local directory are 25 pages, all full of ideas. You can get more information about an idea by a visit to your nearest commercial library. There is one in every big town or city; your local library will tell you where the nearest one is. That will have a range of trade journals and directories to help you.

We can break up different kinds of businesses into three broad groupings:

GOODS AND SERVICES

Creating goods
This means either setting up a factory unit to produce your goods, or being a manufacturer in the old sense (the word meant make by hand!), creating individual items of art or craft: clothing, furniture, toys, sculpture. In each case you must have (or buy) the necessary artistic or engineering skills. For many activities you also need a reasonable amount of cash at the beginning, to buy premises and equipment. What is more, that money will be tied permanently into the business.

Buying and selling goods
At first glance, this is the most open of the three groupings. Everyone has some experience of buying and selling - or at

least of buying. They may think they do not need much expertise to get involved in many areas of selling. Is that really so? The life of many small shopkeepers is tough, as the competition of the big superstores and multiple chains steadily erodes their potential share of the market. Here again it is often the people with special skills that do best. It may be easy to acquire some of those skills, and there will usually be gaps in what is sold locally. Even so, you still need money that can be tied up in the stock and premises.

Providing services
This is the growth area of the British economy over recent years, especially in such areas as tourism, convenience services (such as fast food), leisure facilities and financial services. Look how the high streets of most towns have changed over the last 20 years. Again, the big organisations have muscled in. But there are still plenty of opportunities to be found, some involving much less initial capital. Often they are services to the big organisations which they find it better to sub-contract out than to do in-house. What is more, as estate agencies have shown, sometimes small firms thrive where big organisations founder.

Which kind of activity are you considering? It should be one that provides a genuine business opportunity, not a passing fashion or work only for a short period. It should be one that uses to the full your own skills and strengths, and needs less of the areas in which you don't have skill. And it should be properly affordable for you. Organising your approach to any of these areas is discussed later in the book. But there are some provisional exercises you can do right now with your idea.

Take a sheet of paper. Write on it what you think will have happened to your area of business ten years from now, no matter whether you succeed or fail. It's not impossible - government and big industry employ people to do just this. For example, how will the makeup of the local community have changed? If the prices of houses locally have been pricing out the youngsters with local jobs, what will the community be like in a few years' time? Let's have a look at what those changes might be.

THE TEN YEAR TEST

In most areas there will be more elderly people. The whole country is going steadily greyer over the next 20 years. More of us will survive to over 80. In most areas, there will be fewer people leaving school and in their young twenties, but more of them will stay on at school or college longer. There will be more children of younger school age, though this will vary from area to area. New houses bought by young couples will, in ten years, have children in them. The slightly older estates now have lots of children in them. In ten years' time most of the children will have left home, and the local schools will be a lot emptier. Other, subtler, changes are occurring because of the price of housing and the increasing mobility of the population. People are less integrated and more separated, for example, into middle-class areas, than once was the case. They travel more and have a wider experience of, and often also expectation of, life. For example, they travel abroad much more, and are more likely to have some knowledge of foreign languages and cultures. Equally, many more tourists come here.

HOW THINGS WILL
CHANGE

THE JOB MARKET

There will be more people retiring from work than coming into the labour market for the first time towards the end of this century. There will therefore be shortages of skilled workers, particularly professionals, in a few years' time. Indeed, the shortage is already happening in some areas. Some businesses and professions are already worried about that. How many children will be leaving school or college in your area in each of the next few years? The schools know that. Should you? How will work patterns have changed in the next ten years? Will the shift towards part-time employment and people working from their own homes continue? It has been made more possible by computers, faxes and the other inventions of information technology. Will the shake-out of jobs caused by the increasing inroads of technology into clerical work continue? Will the thinning out of management structures and 'empowerment' prove a passing fad or a permanent shift in employment?

HOW PEOPLE BEHAVE

People will be healthier and will have more leisure time. They will probably smoke and drink less, and eat better food. Some will still be retiring younger, but all will be living longer. Will this spare time, and the free time of the unemployed and underemployed, mean that the crime rate goes on climbing as it has done in recent years? If so, how will people react to that? What else will people do with their leisure? Will the promise of still cheaper air travel mean that everyone has three holidays abroad, where not so long ago they had one week at Blackpool?

Wealthier people (and for this purpose I mean most of us - the majority of households who own their own homes) will get wealthier. This is because, for the first time, as older people die, they leave their increasingly valuable homes to their families. But, unlike previous generations, those families also already own their own homes. Will they use their second homes as holiday homes, or rent them out, or sell them and reinvest the money in something else - either savings or higher consumer spending? Again, serious study of the effects of this shift is already going on. It is assumed that the result in part will be greatly increased savings. Where will the savings go?

These things are not guesswork. We already know they are going to happen. They are the inevitable consequences (catastrophes apart) of trends already happening, and the effects in the future of new discoveries and practices.

WHAT WILL HAPPEN IN YOUR AREA?

With a bit of detective work, you can do a lot more guessing about the future in your area. If there is a new motorway or road improvement planned, what will its effect be when it is opened? The effect of the M25, or of the electrification of lines into Liverpool Street Station, has been enormous in those areas. So is the growth of Manchester International Airport, which went on growing even when some tried to stop it. And it will go on growing. What opportunities will that provide?

What will be the effect of the Channel Tunnel, and the removal of internal barriers in the European Community which took place in 1992? On the other hand, the number of people employed on the land in ordinary farming activities is still dropping. It now forms only a negligible (but still over-producing) sector of a country that not so long ago was a land of farmers. The same is true of mining, shipbuilding and steel, so the towns that used to depend on these businesses are still declining. The decline in the number of small shops goes on relentlessly, as two-car households find it ever easier to drive to their local hypermarket.

HI-TECH AND LOW-TECH

Think what technology is doing. Take this book, for example. It was written on a hard-disk word processor, with a memory big enough to store the whole of this and several other books. When I started writing the first edition, it was with a manual typewriter. The change in the technology of writing and publishing is enormous. That is one small part of the information technology revolution.

Don't get too fascinated by high-tech, though. Many inventions that have affected us most seem low-tech, like cling-wrap and plastic bags, cassette players and car parts that don't need servicing every three weeks. I've said enough to make my point. There should be quite a lot you can already put down on paper. Once we have looked at the information available to you elsewhere (see 'What are you selling?') there will be more.

THINK AS AN ENTREPRENEUR

Why? Entrepreneurs are innovators. They are the people that spot, or as often as not create, new markets and new customers. Think what is on the market now that was not available ten years ago. Who put it there? Many of these developments involve little new - what's new in a hamburger this century? Nor was the work done by the inventor - as British history sadly shows time and again. Rather, someone else came along and persuaded us we needed this 'new' product, to his benefit. Take, for example, a new idea being chased by those selling software: technowant. It is the desire of people to have software on their computers because they think they need it, even though they will never use it.

Quite often, the entrepreneurs were the ones who stopped and thought through the changes that were about to take place in their business. Sometimes they chased the changes that should have taken place, but had not.

Sometimes it is all too obvious. As small shops have given way to large shops, so stores have been staffed, in their customers' views, either by no one at all or by shop assistants who ignore or are rude to the customers. Big has meant anonymous. Many people like a friendly shop. Hence a belated move has got staff in big stores to be as friendly as they used to be in the successful local store. The stores where assistants were recruited and trained to help the customer, or where they don't mind you bringing the clothes back if they don't fit, are doing well. Aren't they?

Sometimes, on a much smaller scale, the entrepreneur is the one who spotted a gap in the local market for a product or service and supplied it. If it is done well enough, it is not worth anyone else's while competing, even if there are many customers for the product or service. Our local specialist cheese shop was like that - and every Saturday morning there is a queue out through the door despite the speed at which his four assistants work. I originally wrote that as part of the first edition. Two editions later, the queues are still there!

WHERE DO YOU COME IN?

The kind of business or opportunity you seize should make the most of your strengths and available resources. It should also be one that suits the lifestyle you want to lead. What kind of commitment do you want to make to your business? In terms of both time and training this may vary enormously. Think of the different hours kept by offices and shops in your own locality. There are sedate offices that only keep 'office hours' - which sometimes seems to mean hardly any at all. And there are the corner shops that are always open. Consider the hours worked by the manager of your local pub - or the time in the morning when the local newsagent or greengrocer start work.

If you are willing to be committed to a business for those hours, you have a valuable asset at your disposal. If not, you may be planning self-imposed imprisonment. Again, the demands during the day will vary enormously. The newsagent's work is largely done by the time the rest of us emerge, until the evening newsround. The launderette, on the other hand, needs to be open all day every day, but only needs close attention when there are problems. Those prepared to offer emergency services - for which premium prices are charged - need constantly to be ready, but get well paid for it.

WHAT ELSE DO YOU DO?

Many people consider working on their own to fit in with other all-consuming interests: sports activities, art or music, or something else which by itself will not earn a living. If that is what you are planning, think about the varying demands of the business you choose through the week and year. How does that fit in with your other plans? Most businesses are seasonal, just as are most hobbies. Do the two go together? There is a season for just about everything. It varies from toy-makers and toyshops (which have to make their profits in the hectic scramble before Christmas) to building (which is always slackest when the toyshops are at their busiest).

Even when you know your own strengths and weaknesses, and have an area of business in mind, there is still much more to think about. The main thing you need to do is to work out your business plan. As part of that, you need to be thinking how best you can start in the business.

TAKING THE PLUNGE

One point merits immediate thought. Should you start your new venture whole-time or part-time? Can you start your business in the evenings and weekends, keeping your main job going until you do not need it any more? This is even more worth considering when the business is a family venture. Can one of you keep working (or start work at a reliable job) while the other one works at the business? You don't have to keep on your present job to do this - there might be other less demanding opportunities around.

PART-TIMING

Keeping a regular source of income while you get started on your own business makes considerable sense if you can do it. There will be no need for quite the same desperate panic if your new venture is slower getting off the ground than you thought. If it proves to be a mistake, you still have another source of revenue to fall back on. How far you can do this varies from one business to another. Sometimes you need to devote your whole time and effort from the beginning if it is going to be a success.

Many successful small businesses were started really small, and only became full-time businesses when the work warranted it. Others will, or should, expect always to remain so unless they are unusually successful. This is particularly true of art and craft industries, where customers are notoriously reluctant to pay the real going rate for a painting or hand-crafted toy or furniture.

Combining two jobs has become much easier in recent years. Required hours of full-time jobs in many sectors of the economy have become shorter, with less compulsory overtime being worked. There are also many more part-time jobs available in the labour market, and opportunities to job-share. Flexibility of work has also greatly increased.

There is another side to this story. In some areas of business, you need to be available at all times right from the start. Customers will not wait just because you ask them. They will go off to your competitors. You may find it hard to get your business going while also directing even a little of your attention to keeping your boss quiet.

NEW ENTERPRISE ALLOWANCES

If you are not in employment, and do not find any suitable work, other help is available for you under the Government's New Enterprise Allowance Scheme, run for the Department of Employment. Each pays between £20 and £90 a week for a year to those who are on unemployment benefit or income support to help them get started on their new job. Otherwise, if they start work, they lose social security entitlement immediately.

If you want to claim an allowance, check with

your local Job Centre, Local Enterprise Agency
or TEC (see the section on outside help).

3   *Setting up a company*

*A*T AN EARLY STAGE in setting up your business you must decide what structure the business will have. If you go it alone you will be a **sole proprietor**. If there are two or more of you, you can form a **partnership** or **cooperative**, or one of you can employ the others, or you can keep your interests separated and trade in parallel. Alternatively, you can turn the business into a **company**. If you do this, the business belongs to the company not you, although you may be the managing director.

In planning this, there are two key decisions. First, are there - or should there be - two or more people involved together in the business? The other person could be your wife, husband, or good friend, someone lending you money, or a former work colleague. Whoever it is, you both need to sort out your working relationships fully at the start. Second, don't rush off and turn the business into a company without thinking why. It could be a costly mistake.

It is one of our less trumpeted liberties that we may set up our own businesses, and stand or fall by our own abilities, without a state licence to do so. Consumer protection measures and other laws mean it is not quite as simple as that these days, but it is the government's avowed aim to keep red tape to a minimum. The government makes a standing request of you. If you have suggestions for getting rid of red tape, send them to the **Enterprise and Deregulation Unit.**

When you set up, check if you need any permission to carry on that business at that place (see 'Location'). In an increasing number of businesses you also need either a qualification or a licence. For example, although anyone can call themselves an accountant, not everyone can give insurance or legal advice, nor can they call themselves a bank.

One problem is that local rules often vary. You may need local permission to open a coffee shop as well as an off-licence. The need for taxi licences is well known, but less so is the need for licences for nursing homes - though local councils deal with both. Tobacconists need a licence, while newspapers should be registered with the Post Office..., and so the list goes on. There are hundreds of different licensing requirements. Many are administered by local councils. Check with your local enterprise agency, the local TEC, the local council or your professional advisers to see what requirements there are affecting your business. There will almost certainly be some, if only your duty to tell the tax authorities.

Choosing the right name is vital. How open is the choice? You can conduct business under

THE SOLE TRADER

CHOOSING THE BUSINESS NAME

your own name (perhaps with the suffix '& Co' added - that makes no legal difference). But you may decide on another name. If you use any name other than your own surname, perhaps together with your own forename or initials, you must comply with the **Business Names Act**. This requires you to put your own name, and your address, on all business letters, written orders for goods or services, invoices and receipts and written demands for payment of business debts. Failure to do so is an offence for which people can be fined.

Don't pinch someone else's name. They can object to your name if they can show you are **passing-off** your business as theirs. If your business is the same as or too similar to that of another business, the result may be that their customers might confuse the two businesses. If so, court action could be taken against you to prevent you using that name and also to get damages from you. Major companies are particularly aggressive in protecting their names in this way.

Logos (like the BMW sign on cars) are protected **trade marks**, and pictures, music, special phrases ('It's finger-lickin' good') are protected **copyright**. All belong to their owners just as much as other kinds of property. You should not use them for your business without permission. That is one of the key aspects of a franchise agreement. And remember, if you get a good logo, name, phrase or design, you can protect it too, though you should seek legal advice about it.

IN BUSINESS TOGETHER   **Married (and other) couples** - We have seen that if one of a couple goes into business, it should be with the other's support. In practice, the other will inevitably be involved in some way. Does that mean both should be partners in the business, or one should employ the other? It may mean that one of the couple does the work while the other puts up the money. At the other extreme, it may mean that the partner going into business thinks it wise to transfer his interest in the family home and other property to the other partner. I recall one divorcee ruefully remarked to me that it was swapping a bad risk for a worse one! For myself, I don't agree, but there are some serious issues to be thought about.

If the couple both work at a business without reaching an agreement, custom might regard the business as the husband's. The law would not agree - for tax, social security, family law and other purposes the business will normally be jointly that of husband and wife, and profits should be shared equally. If the couple want it some other way, they should agree otherwise. If the wife is playing a small part in the business, it may be better that she is an employee (see 'Employees').

The business may also put the family home at risk. If a lender wants it as security for, say, the husband's loan, the wife will usually be asked to agree. This is because, although the husband is sole owner of the house, the wife has rights to live there. These rights take priority over those of a lender. If the husband defaults on his loan, and the wife has not agreed to the loan because, for example, she had never heard of it, the mortgagee cannot sell the house unless the court agrees.

There are several ways that people can go into business together. One can agree to put up the

OTHERS WORKING
TOGETHER

money while another does the work. The one putting up the money need not be involved in the other's business, and can merely be an investor. Often, lenders want a say in how the business runs. In that case lender and borrower must get together either through a partnership (where the lender will be a 'sleeping partner', see below) or a company, where the lender will be a shareholder and, probably, director.

In other cases, two or more people will work side by side in the same business. There is a lot to be gained by arranging to work together with others in a team helping each other. If all have a share in the business, they have to become a partnership or a cooperative or jointly form a company in which all have a stake. By some route they must determine who runs the business, and what share each has in it. If there is no agreement but the team goes ahead anyway, the law will treat the team as being equal partners.

PARTNERSHIPS

A business partnership may come into existence like an arranged marriage, with proper attention to formality and detail. Or it may happen like a love affair. Only when the euphoria has worn off, and problems become apparent, do you realise what has happened.

The law requires no formalities of a business partnership. Partners may have introduced considerable amounts of money into the business, or none at all. A partnership exists, to quote the law, whenever two or more persons 'carry on business in common with a view to profit'. If people jointly run a business, sharing business decisions, sharing profits and the risk of losses, and working together, they will be partners. The law imposes rights and duties on them as partners to each other unless and until they agree otherwise. Whatever they agree, one or more of the partners must be personally liable for all partnership debts. If the business fails, those partners will lose out completely.

Agreement is most important. The law lays down rules in the Partnership Acts that govern partnerships, but all these rules can be changed by agreement. That is why partners should always draw up an agreement with proper advice to set your own rules. If you do not, the rules laid down by law are those set out below. Do not assume, because you are good friends before the partnership, that you will make good business colleagues, or even stay friends.

PARTNERS' RIGHTS AND DUTIES

Unless you agree otherwise, partners are equally entitled to share in profits and are equally at risk for the losses. What is more, each partner is responsible for the full debts of the partnership, so a creditor can sue any of them. Each partner also has full authority to act as agent for all other partners, and to pledge the credit of all partners for the business. Further, a former partner may remain responsible for partnership debts after leaving the partnership. The tax position will depend on the separate earnings of the partners, as well as their joint earnings.

Partners can leave the partnership, and withdraw their capital at will without notice, unless otherwise agreed. No provision is made for a partner who has an accident or reaches retirement age. Decisions on matters such as this have to be joint decisions. In many cases each partner has an effective right of veto. Failure to foresee problems like this may result in financial loss to some partners.

It is quite common to have a partnership where some of those involved are **sleeping partners.** These are partners whose money is involved in the business, and who may have some decision-making powers, but who are not concerned with the management and day-to-day running of the business. Their money is in the business as an investment. It is also possible to have **limited partnerships**, where some partners are sleeping partners whose capital is at risk but who, under the partnership terms, are liable to lose only that capital, and do not have unlimited liability. In either case at least one partner must be a **general partner** with unlimited liability for debts.Normally, where such kinds of arrangements are wanted, companies have provided an easier way of doing it.

Partnership Agreements : a checklist

It will pay to get your agreement drawn up properly by a solicitor in all but the simplest case. Here are some problems the agreement should cover :

When does the partnership start?

Where is it to be carried on?

What is the business of the partnership?

Can it carry on any other business?

Who are the partners? Are they all general partners? Who is the senior partner?

Can other people become partners, and if so, do all the existing partners have to be in favour?

How much capital is each partner bringing into the partnership?

Will the partnership have its own business premises, or will these belong to one or more partners ?

What is the position with partnership equipment, cars, etc?

How much interest will the partnership pay each year on the capital? How much rent for the premises, cars, and so on?

Who is responsible for making contracts for the partnership?

Who signs the cheques and who keeps the books? Does any one partner have unlimited authority to do these things, or do bigger contracts or cheques need signing by two or more partners?

How much time will each partner spend in the business?

What holidays are allowed? What happens if a partner is ill?

Are partners allowed to carry on any other business at the same time?

Who hires and fires the staff? How are other important decisions to be reached?

What happens if there is a dispute between the partners?

How long does the partnership last?

What happens if a partner wants to retire?

Do the other partners pay a pension?

How much notice is needed to leave the partnership, or to take capital out?

What happens if one partner dies?

A final point: when someone leaves a partnership, all the customers and suppliers have to be notified. Otherwise the former partner may still be liable for partnership debts, and the new partners for his debts. Also, a badly timed breakup of a partnership may significantly increase the tax payable by the partners. For both reasons, it is worth getting proper advice at the end of a partnership as well as the beginning.

COOPERATIVES

Cooperatives are somewhere between employment and self-employment. They are businesses where, technically, the workforce are all employees of the cooperative, but where the same people are also the employer. In many partnerships, as in a company, some of those involved are more equal than others. In a cooperative everyone is genuinely equal. They are all running their own business even though, inevitably, they have different jobs to do within the business. Some cooperatives are very small. Others can be national businesses.

Cooperatives sometimes emerge when businesses are to close but the staff agree to club together (often pooling redundancy money) to buy the business from the employer and run it jointly. Quite often members are pulled together by a common ideal in the true workers cooperative. ICOM, the Industrial Common Ownership Movement (address at end) exists to encourage worker cooperatives, and helps with information, and access to finance. Cooperatives need to register and adopt certain formalities, and ICOM helps with these.

A government agency, the Cooperative Development Agency (address at end) promotes the interests of cooperatives, with limited powers to make grants and loans. In some areas there are also local cooperative development agencies, often supported by local councils, and they may be the best place for help if near you. Find out through the CDA.

COMPANIES

There are several kinds of company, including unlimited companies, and companies limited by guarantee. Only one sort is important to the small business, the company limited by shares or Co Ltd as we normally say. A plc (public limited company) is the special status for the large publicly owned company, which we ignore here.

The key to a limited company is that the company belongs to the people who have shares in it, or its shareholders. Their liability is to the company, not its customers, for the full value of the shares, and no more. The crucial difference between running a business as a sole trader or through a partnership, and through a company is that in law the company is separate from those who own it. It is the company, not the company's owners, which runs the business. This means that if the business fails, the company fails but not its shareholders. They lose only the value of the shares. That, at any rate, is the theory. In practice, it doesn't quite work that simply in most cases, because banks and other lenders demand personal guarantees from those running the business.

HOW IS A COMPANY
FORMED?

A company can be set up only through the Companies Registration Office (address at end). To register a company, the intending shareholders must draw up and file a series of documents setting out the company's rules, and details about it and its owners. The key documents of any company are :

The Memorandum setting out the company's 'vital statistics'. These must include:

Its name

Its country of registration (England or Scotland)

The objects and purposes of the business

Total value of the share capital.

The Articles of Association setting out the company's rules.

This can be a long, complex document, but often follows (in a standard form laid down as in **Table A**), rules laid down under the Companies Act 1985, the main law on companies. If it does this, the document can be less than a page long.

Along with these documents, the Registration Office must receive the name(s) of the first **directors** and secretary of the company. All companies must have either two directors or a director and a company secretary. There must also be **subscribers**, people who agree to buy at least one share each. A company must always have one or more shareholders - though one can be a nominee of another (for instance the main shareholder's solicitor), so that one-owner companies are easily set up. Under recent changes of the law, a company can be owned by one shareholder alone, so the second shareholder that used to be necessary can back out.

The company's **name** must be different from that of any other company. Have some spare names at hand. A name can be changed once the company is in existence but the country of registration cannot be changed.

The company's **objects** are vital, as these set the legal limits to the powers of the company's management to carry on business. Action outside the company's powers is said to be beyond its powers or **ultra vires**. A company can sometimes refuse to carry out a contract made in excess of its actual powers. This is usually so where a company makes an ultra vires agreement with its owners and directors, and can create serious problems for the owners if a company becomes insolvent or gets into the hands of others. However, companies can now be set up with the object of being a 'general commercial company'. This means that the problems about the company's powers can be avoided. Otherwise, the objects need to be drafted with care.

The company's **rules** are usually of little concern to outsiders, but are as important as the partnership agreement to the owners and directors. Many of the questions in the partnership checklist will also apply to setting limits to the directors' powers and duties, and the holding of meetings. There will also be rules about selling the company's shares - usually preventing outsiders getting hold of company shares without agreement of at least a majority of existing shareholders.

You can set up a company by buying one 'off

the shelf'. They are advertised regularly in the business press for about £150 or so. It may be wiser to get either your solicitor or a company registration agent to set one up to your requirements. Get them to explain the legal requirements of a company for you. The Companies Act lays down in considerable detail the rights and duties of the directors, shareholders, company secretary and others, and requires regular **annual returns** of information about the company.

RUNNING A COMPANY

Once the registration certificate is issued, the subscribers take up their shares to become shareholders, and the company holds its first meeting to appoint one or more directors and a secretary. It is then required to elect company auditors (the business's accountants do this), and select a registered office (usually the accountants' or solicitors' office). After that it is in business.

One of these formalities is to be removed in 1994. At present all companies must appoint a company auditor and must allow the auditor to audit the company's annual accounts. The government has announced plans to abolish this requirement for small companies - those with profits less than £90,000. They will not need to produce annual accounts unless their shareholders require it. They will, however, still need to produce adequate accounts for tax and VAT purposes.

Just as a company's formation has to follow a set form by law, so does its running. The company is required to have an **AGM** for its shareholders within 18 months of the start, and at least every 15 months afterwards. These meetings must receive (and hopefully approve) reports from the directors and auditors, and elect directors and the auditors. **Annual reports** must include summaries of the accounts, names of the directors, details about the shareholders, and other information. Further, a copy of these details must be filed each year as an **annual return** to the Companies Registration Office. There they are open to public inspection, and will be monitored and scrutinised by potential rivals and predators.

This may seem a lot of formality for a small business, but these legal requirements cannot be ignored. This is because the company is, from incorporation, a separate legal person. It is also advisable if there are two or more people involved to keep proper, if short, minutes of all formal decisions of the directors and meetings, including time, place and the signatures of those attending.

It is difficult to keep the company's affairs separate from those of its owner in what is in effect a one-person business. However, company property must be kept separate from shareholders' property. It must trade in its own name, not its owner's. It must keep separate bank accounts, books and contracts. Its owner will be an employee for income tax and social security purposes (see 'Tax') if he or she works for the business, even as managing director and sole employee. As we shall see below, the owner can instead take out the money as dividends on the shares. The best way for this to happen will depend in part on taxation questions.

KEEPING THE
COMPANY SEPARATE

WHAT FORM OF
BUSINESS?

There are both advantages and disadvantages in running a business through a company rather than a partnership. As a result, there is no one clear answer as to what form a business should adopt. Obviously, the big businesses are nearly always companies (apart from accountants and lawyers, who are not allowed as yet to be incorporated). The very smallest businesses will often find the corporate form formal, inflexible, and expensive.

The following is a checklist of points for you to consider :

Setting up

Should involve formality for a partnership.
Must involve formalities and official fees for a company.
Nothing required for a sole trader.

Running costs

Minimal for a partnership.
None for a sole trader.
A company must throughout comply with all legal requirements.

Changing your mind

While it is fairly easy to turn an unincorporated business into a company, the reverse is not true. It can be very expensive to disincorporate for tax reasons - so don't rush into forming a company on a short-term basis.

Image

Don't be taken in by the glamour of being a company director - others won't be. But in some areas of activity the business may look a more serious endeavour if incorporated.

Secrecy

A partnership reports nothing, except to the partners.

A company has to publish part of its accounts and other key details (although this is limited for very small companies).

Accounts and auditing

Company accounts must be officially audited (subject to changes for the smallest companies), while there are no requirements imposed on partnership accounts for outsiders.

Borrowing money

It is easier for a company to raise money than a partnership, whose main source will be loans. Companies can get investments through selling some shares, and there are tax schemes to help this, or by raising money by a floating charge (see 'Raising finance').

Limited liability

There is no limit to the liability of general partners of a partnership, or of sole traders. In principle, the shareholders of a limited company risk only their invested capital. In practice, banks, landlords and others will demand personal guarantees from the company's owners.

Tax

There are several different tax reasons why you may wish to be or not to be a company - summarised below

Social Security

Because all those in a company are

treated as employees they pay the higher Class 1 contributions. Partners pay Classes 2 and 4, as do sole traders.

Selling or passing on your interest

Because the company is legally separate from its owners it is easier to sell the business, especially part of it, or to pass a share in the business to other members of the family for personal or tax reasons.

For small businesses it is often better for tax reasons not to be incorporated. Among the relevant factors are :

Income Tax

Employees (and directors) of a company pay tax on their earnings through PAYE and under the less generous rules applying to all employees. Perks such as company cars do not now save tax to the extent they used to.

Tax rates

A company pays flat rate tax at 25 per cent (rising to 33 per cent if its profits exceed £300,000) on all its profits (including any capital gains). If it keeps its profits, that is all that is paid.

If it pays its profits out as dividends, it has to account for ACT (Advance Corporation Tax) at the rate of 20 per cent of the total paid out to the Revenue. However, this is treated as paying tax on the dividend in the hands of the individual shareholder. If the shareholder is liable to higher rate tax, there will be a further 20 per cent to pay. If not, there is no more to pay. Because the ACT can be set off against the tax bill of the company, this means, in effect, the company pays very little tax (effectively about 6 per cent). If the company pays its profits out as earnings, then the ACT is avoided, as is the tax on profits, but NI contributions become payable (at 10.2 per cent in most cases).

Partners and sole traders pay tax at 25 per cent and 40 per cent, with Class 2 (flat rate) and Class 4 (7.3 per cent on a slice only of the profits) NI contributions as well.

National Insurance Contributions

These are much higher for directors and employees, and include the employer's contribution and the Class 1A contribution on company cars and free fuel. This may be avoided to some extent by paying dividends to the owners rather than earnings. However, payment of earnings can be used as a basis for pension contribution payments, and these can be set off against liability to pay contributions as an employee to some extent, as well as being deductible against income before tax. Dividends cannot be used as a basis for pension contributions.

Capital gains

This works one way only. Companies and their owners get taxed twice on capital gains. The company pays on making the gain. But this increases the share value to the owner, who will pay capital gains tax on selling or giving the shares on that gain. If, say, a gain by the company is taxed in the hands of the company then the rate is 25 per cent. The balance of the capital gain realised goes to increase the share value. If the shares are sold while including this value, then the increase in share price will be taxed at (probably) 40 per cent – an effective further tax on the original gain of 30 per cent, making 55 per cent in total.

This can be reduced by exemptions,

but such a position is better avoided. Exemptions are granted for shares in family companies as well as for sole-owned businesses.

Stamp Duty

There is a 1 per cent stamp duty on all sales of shares. There is no stamp duty in moving partners' capital into or out of a partnership.

Inheritance Tax and tax planning

It is far easier to make gifts of shares to reduce inheritance tax liabilities than move a share of an unincorporated business. Tax reliefs for businesses apply both to companies and partnerships or sole trading businesses.

4 *Plan it*

*I*f you don't know where you're going, you won't get there. Before you set out, it is vital that you know your objectives, and that you think about how to attain them. Whatever your business, big or small, you must have clear objectives, and a **business plan** setting out how to achieve them. If you don't, you will probably fail to achieve your aims. Your business may fail altogether. People rarely plan to fail, but they often fail to plan.

A business plan enables you to decide what to do about achieving your objectives. To do this, it must be thorough and cover all aspects of what you are doing. That's why much of this book is concerned with aspects of your planning. But the highlights of your plan will be the **five Ps.**

P URPOSE

P RODUCT

P OTENTIAL

P EOPLE

P OUNDS

What is the aim of your business? What are your objectives in setting it up? This is the core of your plan. For larger organisations, this is sometimes given the grand name of a **mission statement**, a formal recognition of what the organisation is for. Your statement does not need to be grand. It needs only to be accurate. Write your aims down in a short, simple statement - six or seven lines may suffice. It should answer the vital issues: where is your business going? Why?

This is crucial to your planning, because it states your principal objectives. It also challenges you to channel your energies into those objectives. The remainder of the plan is your proposed ways of achieving the target. That should help prevent you from being side-tracked into irrelevant activities. These merely waste your most valuable resource - you.

Don't be afraid of having to alter the aims later. If you are successful, you will probably need to do so at some point. In any event, you should reconsider the aims every few months to see if they should be revised, or if you should refocus on them. As your business develops, so your targets will change.

Only you can set that purpose. Why not have a first try now:

The main objective of my business is:

....

....

....

....

....

....

....

....

PRODUCT

Whatever your business, you must be supplying a product to someone. If you are to succeed, there must be some special reason why *your* product is worth getting. Write those into a **product description** in your plan for each product you aim to produce. Your plan needs to provide three more Ps for each product:

Product price
Product plan
Product procurement

PRODUCT PRICE

All products have a unit cost, that is, the cost of producing one item (or for a service, this may be cost per hour of service). Working this out is part of the market planning we examine below.

PRODUCT PLAN

You must also plan the development of the product, and how it will be kept marketable. Each product, like your whole business, and everything else, has its own life cycle. This will follow the form:

Birth
Growth
Maturity
Decline

Your business, and each product of it, follows this pattern. Your plan should aim to support the earlier stages for each product, so that decline is postponed. When it comes, the business should have other products at earlier stages of their lives, so the business itself continues to grow.

Decline, when it comes, may be sudden. It may

hit your product just when it wipes out a whole industry. If you are tied to one product, you go when it goes. Don't turn into a dinosaur. Aim for a portfolio of products to protect your business against this threat. If you don't think it a threat, look what happened to the Swiss watch industry a few years ago (until Swatch was invented), or the British coalmining industry...

Next, you must plan how you can supply your product to your customers. You need to analyse the work involved in preparing everything so that the product is delivered at the right time, place and price. This is your job. But what exactly is it you must do?

PRODUCT
PROCUREMENT

Work out a chart, a **Work Breakdown Structure**, of what needs doing, first by the main kinds of activity involved, then splitting down each area of activity. This helps you in planning and then monitoring the business, spotting weak points in your organisation. Try something resembling the example on the next page.

Along the bottom of your work breakdown structure should be a list of all the activities in which you need to engage to get your product to the market. Does this cover all you should be doing? Have irrelevant activities crept in?

Work Breakdown Structure: The Small Building Co.

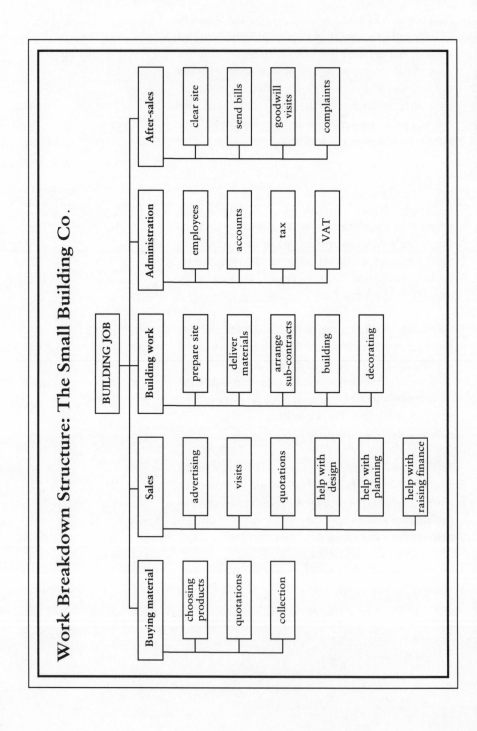

Next, you can turn this into a time-organising chart. Each activity in developing your product takes time. What is that time? Can you write it down? Some of those activities must take place before others can be started. Some, by contrast, can be done at the same time as others. Some come at the end. What is the best order for them?

If your business involves a chain of activities (as all manufacturing does), a good way of tracing the timing of the activities is to chart them on a **network plan**. One way of doing this is shown on the chart on the next page. Each activity is represented by a line with circles showing where the activity begins and is finished. The length of the line indicates the time spent on the activity.

This chart gives you other vital information: the length of time each job will take. It shows what is called the **critical path**, the shortest time between the beginning and end of the job. If anything in the critical path goes wrong, the whole job is delayed. Shorten the critical path, and the job gets finished quicker. Pay careful attention to every aspect of your business on the critical path, and plan to keep them all as short as possible.

The plan also tells you in what order you should be doing things. The aim is to order things so as to shorten the critical path as much as possible. You may delay non-critical parts of the business. This is particularly important to avoid tying up cash until you need to do so. When do you need to buy your stock and equipment? Aim to get them **'just in time'**.

TIME IT RIGHT

Network chart: Wibble Widgets Ltd – batch of custom-designed widgets

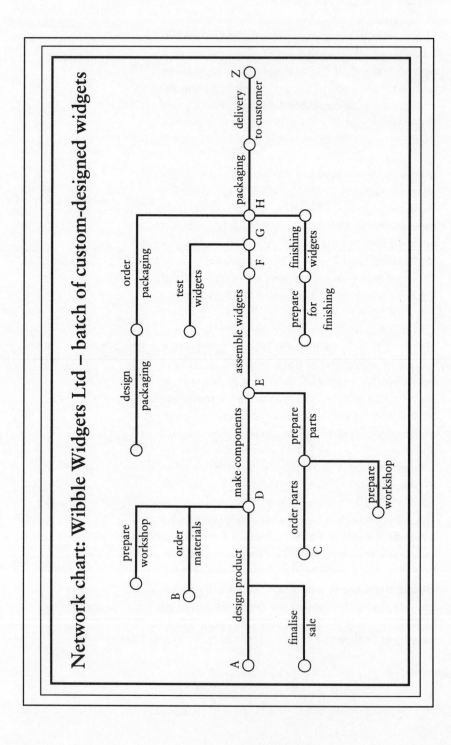

The principle of 'just in time' is to reduce to a minimum the time during which equipment and materials - and people - are left standing idle before or between jobs. If materials are delivered too early, the business may suffer in several ways. You have to pay for the stock too soon. You have to find storage space for it, and run the risk of damage, theft and deterioration while it is lying idle. Getting the stock just in time demands two things of the business - good planning and good suppliers. If the planning is right, it may be cheaper to pay a little more for reliable stock delivery than to go for cheaper supplies that are hoarded 'just in case'.

The same principle applies to staff time - is that left lying around, or do staff get on with a second job as the first one finishes?

'JUST IN TIME'

Your plan must explore how your business is to go on growing. If it stops growing, it will be mature and will then decline. This involves market research and product development as discussed above and again later in the book. The business plan should include targets for growing in either of the ways shown there - by expanding the product range to existing customers, or expanding the customer base. It should also be looking to improve the efficiency of the business within its existing product range and customer base. This will tend to happen in any event as the business moves from the birth phase to the growth phase, but should be monitored carefully.

POTENTIAL

Another part of the plan is you and the other people involved in the business. As the business

PEOPLE

grows, so will the number of people involved. You need to recruit with care, and plan who does what in the business. Everyone in the team will also need to be managed. Remember, they are your biggest asset next to yourself. They should therefore be given the opportunity to contribute their maximum to the business, and to get the maximum out of it.

POUNDS

The other element vital to your business plan is the cash. You must plan thoroughly all the financial aspects of your business. This involves budgeting ahead for the capital needed to start up the business, and for the cash flow position of the business month by month (see below). You should also be budgeting for the projected profits of the business based on your objectives. This should include the potential you aim to exploit in the coming year (also discussed below). Finally, you should work out the actual and estimated unit costs of your products.

All these financial projections of the business together give you a good picture of what is supposed to be happening. Your records and management accounting have the purpose of making sure you stay on target. If you are missing the target, they should alert you to the change so that you can take corrective action.

CASH FLOW

Cash flow means the money coming into and going out of the business week by week. Most businesses are seasonal. Therefore, unlike a wage packet, profits will come in unevenly. Perhaps a large customer refrains from paying for two months. The bills come in unevenly too. Problems arise the moment bills have to be paid faster than profits come in - as far too many small builders learn to their cost. It is no good knowing that you will make a huge profit when you complete a new house if you can't afford to pay the tiler to finish the roof.

It is absolutely fundamental to every business - and all personal expenditure too - that cash flow must always be in control. Once it gets out of control, disaster awaits. Far too many businesses fail during the first three years for this reason. Basic advance planning reduces this risk.

What you need is a **cash flow forecast** - more work for your pencil! There's an example below. This shows what can go wrong. You can usually get blank forms for your own forecast from your local bank, and you can easily build one up on a computer spreadsheet. Otherwise, adapt the basic form used here.

Flo's Angling Supplies: cash flow forecast
(from start in May)

	May	June	July	August
STARTING BALANCE	0	(9600)	(6800)	(4400)
Income :				
cash sales	2000	3000	5000	5000
credit sales	-	2000	4000	4000
capital receipts	-	10000	-	-
other income	200	400	400	800
Total income	**2200**	**15400**	**9400**	**9800**
Outgoings :				
cash purchases	400	200	200	200
credit purchases	4000	1000	1000	-
wages etc	2000	2000	2000	2000
rent and rates	2000	2000	2000	2000
running premises	600	-	600	-
repairs etc	2000	-	-	-
running equipment	400	400	400	400
travel	200	400	200	200
capital purchases	-	6000	-	-
loan payments	-	400	400	400
other expenses	200	200	200	200
Total expenses	**11800**	**12600**	**7000**	**5400**
BALANCE for month	**(9600)**	**2800**	**2400**	**440**
CLOSING BALANCE	**(9600)**	**(6800)**	**(4400)**	**0**

It is a standard practice in accounts to put negative figures in brackets, so we can see Flo's business is getting steadily into the red.

Flo's projections show that she has no ready cash until August, and is heavily in the red for three months. How could she have avoided this without in any way increasing her income? What would have happened if she had secured the loan a month earlier, and had put off some of the expenditure (eg the capital items and repairs) for a couple of months? This is a simple example, but when you have your own cash flow projection, look at the alternatives it suggests, plus the amount of start up capital needed.

You should also be looking ahead to your intended profit level. This is a separate exercise to the cash flow forecast because the profits calculation is based on earnings, rather than when cash comes in. You should check this in the same way as cashflow. The aim is to produce a best guess at the profit and loss account for the month, and so on for the current year.

BUDGETING

Have a look at the profit and loss account on page 90 and compare it with the cashflow form. What you need to check here for each month is:

1	Sales (turnover)
2	less cost of sales
3	plus other income
4	GROSS PROFIT (1–2 + 3)
5	less overheads
6	NET PROFIT (4 –5)
7	CUMULATIVE NET PROFIT (totalsof 6 for that and each previous month of the year)

The budget forecast will be different from the cashflow figures. It also emphasises a fundamental difference between the **fixed overheads** and the **variable** (or sales-related) **overheads.** That is important in working out the **break-even point** for the business. This is because you must pay the fixed overheads whatever your sales. But your gross profit on each sale is the difference between the sale proceeds and the cost of that sale. Once you work that out, you know what your minimum sales must be to cover all overheads.

SPOTTING TROUBLE COMING

Clearly the budget must allow for the break-even figure and show a sensible profit as the target. How to get to that target is of course part of the business plan. But you must also check how you are actually doing compared with the budget. Then you must roll the whole process forward every month. You should also do that with the cash flow forecast. That way you can see as soon as possible if the cash flow or profit predictions are going wrong. And you can take early corrective action.

PUTTING THE PLAN TOGETHER

Once you have planned the five Ps, construct your full business plan to cover everything from your long-term objectives to a detailed monthly estimate of your financial position. You may need two or more business plans. The fullest one is for your use. But when you need to raise money, lenders want to see a business plan, and all the information about purpose, product, potential, people and pounds we explored above. Set out the information you have assembled in preparing your own plan. Start it with a short general description of your business and the market of which your business is part. Prepare the document carefully and you have a good argument why the bank should lend you the money you need.

Because money is so critical to your business, we will discuss it, and your control over it, thoroughly before moving on to other topics. But first, what exactly are you selling?

5   *What are you selling*

I ASK THIS BECAUSE, although it is the wrong question with which to start, many people nonetheless work out a very positive answer to it. They should have been working on their answer to another question. That is :

WHAT CAN YOU
PROVIDE THAT OTHER
PEOPLE WANT TO BUY
AND ARE PREPARED TO
PAY FOR?

The difference between the questions is the difference between **marketing** your business and abilities, and **selling** your existing or intended range of products or services. Sure, you need to sell yourself. That's why a later section is devoted to it. But that still assumes that someone wants to buy what you are selling. Do you know that, and do you know who wants to buy? Just as important, do you know why they want to buy?

Your planning should include much more than deciding how you are going to sell your product. Find out what customers really want, and how much it will cost to give them what they want, then make sure you can get it to them. Only then does the selling start. Before that we must concentrate on market research, product planning and product pricing. This is all more work for your pencil.

By this stage you probably have a fairly clear idea of the line of business you intend to enter - either something you will create or manufacture, or a particular area of sales or supplies of services. Your objective should be to identify what you can supply. Of course, you can perfectly properly start at the other end, without a clear idea, and go looking for something in which to trade. After all, any line of business which produces a profit is a line worth pursuing by someone.

The essence is to realise the range of things that you can provide, and see what will work best. Unless you are a sub-contractor aiming to supply one or a very few main contractors, you have some scope for adjusting what you are doing. If you are an expert you can sell both products and expertise, by becoming the local specialist. Or you can offer extra efficiency or speed in delivery. Or you can go the other way and provide a 'no frills' service.

Generally, small businesses survive on providing that extra 'something' customers want and which big businesses find it much harder or too expensive to supply. That's why it is important to identify the market for which you are catering - and to check it out.

There are two parts to researching your proposed customers :

Library research, that is, tapping the wealth of information available for everything you can find out about your

WELL, WHAT *ARE* YOU SELLING?

RESEARCHING THE MARKET

customers, your competitors, and likely developments amongst both; and

Direct research, or going and finding out.

Whatever specialist market you enter, there is a wealth of published knowledge available about the market just waiting for you to take a systematic look through it. There are two ways to get at this: via your local reference or commercial library, or your local TEC. Some libraries produce special guides to help - and the staff invariably will do so.

Population figures are available from the **Registrar General**'s annual reports, whilst information about spending comes from the annual **Family Expenditure Surveys**. And there is much more. The **Census of Distribution** for your local area will tell you how many similar sorts of shops there are in your area, and what their overall profitability is. And the DTI's **Business Monitors** give regular updates of the state of the market for many different sectors of the economy. A huge range of statistics are available in national or local statistical collections.

You can supplement this data from several sources. There are a large number of commercially prepared directories which will give you all the names and addresses you need for suppliers, competitors, relevant organisations, and so on. Professional organisations and trade associations have membership lists, many of them published. And, of course, there are the telephone directories, **Yellow Pages** being a most valuable reference source.

You should look out for specialist journals, of

which a good commercial library should stock a selection. Find out what journals and papers are available in your trade, and get hold of copies. If you are not sure, check in **British Rate and Data**, which is the list of all journals, papers and periodicals produced for advertisers. There may well also be relevant specialist books in the reference part of the library. Check your nearest business library via the library catalogue (or the library staff).

Another approach to finding out what you want is through **trade exhibitions and conferences**. The specialist exhibitions like the regional Ideal Home exhibitions, or the Business to Business displays give you a splendid chance to see what others are up to, and to talk to both suppliers and customers. That should give you some ideas for selling, as well.

From all these sources, you should be assembling data on what the market looks like, how it is changing, how the national picture is reflected in your region, and what your potential competitors are doing about meeting market demand, and even roughly how much money they are making at it.

If your competitors are companies, you can get more information about them, because (as we have already seen in 'Setting up a company') all companies have to file information about themselves. This is available to you via a **company search** at the Companies Registration Office (commercial agencies do this for you quite cheaply) or, more readily, via the company information services such as Extel which major business libraries carry.

FILE IT

Finally, do not neglect the information you can pick up as you go along, keeping cuttings out of the press, leaflets and advertisements from rivals or information about the customers you intend to serve. Keep that, along with all the other information you have gleaned, in an organised way and it will repay the time spent gathering it.

TEST THE MARKET

Most of the information collected so far can be gained without venturing into the marketplace in any sense (except, anonymously if you wish, at the trade exhibitions). Now go and find out what people want. Ask your friends and contacts. Ask those who you think you will be supplying what they would like. Ask your own intended suppliers what they think. Most people are flattered to be asked their advice. It is paying them a compliment to listen to their experience, and they usually return the compliment by telling you what they think will serve you well.

Depending on what your business is, you can do your own, or commission the experts to do, market research in the well-tried Gallup method of asking organised questions. If that is what you want, it is important to ensure that the questions you ask do not get so loaded that they produce only loaded answers. The questions also need to be targetted to find out what you want to know. In practice that sort of level of research is way beyond what many small businesses need, and beyond their budgets. They can get what they want by systematic desk work backed by listening to those whom they have approached informally.

Once you have started, there will be a steady

source of market information available to you from within your own business. It is vital to keep tabs on that. What are people buying from you, when (time of day/year) do they buy? Are they buying for themselves or others? If you have credit customers, keep a note of all present and past customers, and what they buy. Or keep a check on who comes into your office or shop during a set period, so as to get a full picture.

One of the more recent fashions of management schools and books is the search for total quality management. This emphasises that everything you do is part of what you sell. All aspects of your product should therefore be subject to quality control. This applies as much to replies to letters as it does to your main product. Quality management turns up in a number of guises. One is compliance with BS 5950. This British Standard entitles firms to claim the kitemark for quality control if they reach the required standards in the view of independent assessors.

QUALITY CONTROL

You do not have to go to the lengths of the British Standard to benefit from the key message behind the process of quality management. The names may be new, but the idea is not. It means simply that you try and ensure that what you do is always of top quality. Further, you should establish systems that ensure continuing quality. To do this, attention needs to be given, for example, to the system whereby a customer complaint is handled. Targets should be set, for example, so that all letters from customers should receive an answer within two days. If a full answer cannot be given then, some indication should be given of when it will come. The idea is that the combination of systems and targets, together with continuing review, will ensure full quality delivery every time.

Quality delivery every time should be your aim too. The first step in dealing with this is to regard everything you do as part of the product you are selling. With that in mind, thought needs to be given to how every aspect of your business activities is tackled. Take, for example, the handling of complaints.

COMPLAINTS ARE GOOD FOR YOU

Check what goes wrong even more carefully. Many retailers have gained in market share simply by noting the things people ask for that are not in stock, and spotting additional opportunities. Then look to the complaints. However good you are, you will get complaints and grumbles from customers. You are too slow, too quick, badly stocked, carrying so many lines it is confusing, too dear, too cheap.

We all receive complaints, and we all dislike it. But the wiser people are those who get better because of their mistakes, regarding them as suggestions for improvement rather than personal insults. Few people enjoy complaining (and we soon find out those that do!), so when they complain there is a good reason. If someone complains, how many other customers could have complained but did not? Perhaps the complaint is aimed at your rivals too. There's a new market opportunity.

Don't neglect your staff. They are the people that have to grin stupidly whilst getting roundly cursed because you forgot the customer's order. And they like to have their opinion heard too - what is more, they probably know what they are talking about, and will certainly know what their friends think of your business.

By now your pencil should have done a fair amount of work finding out about the market. Use that to your best advantage by planning how best to exploit the market. You should have a better idea of what people think they want, and what the competition currently offers them.

Think about the demand you are intending to supply from the customer's point of view. Your (or my) literary masterpiece may be viewed by the reader as a reasonably pleasant dose of anaesthetic to ward off the effects of one of British Rail's less efficient services.(It was noticeable, when I was doing some of my own market research, how many business books are now sold through the bookshops at stations and airports - why?) The grotty room at the back of a small hotel on the Costa Grigia will be romanticised into sunshine, cheap booze and scope for late night exercise. The banana peeling machine you so cleverly invented is the way for Fred Ltd to sack an overpaid and unpopular operative.

Within your intended market, there is room for choice. You should know what your competitors are supplying. They will of course react to your presence if they can. How are you going to compete with them and grab your market share? They have the advantage of being there first - or is it a disadvantage? Your research should give you an answer to that. Is their delivery time so unreliable that people will pay more for guaranteed delivery, or is it the sort of place where you pay for excessive attention that most customers don't want, or where they need advice but can't readily get it, or where goods are sometimes faulty, but the supplier is very stroppy when customers ask for money back?

Here again, keep your pencil busy. Work out the

PRODUCT PLANNING

options, and the different levels at which you could supply the market. And if you supply them with one thing, why not with other compatible goods or services? Remember, too, the point about total quality control. Has your planning covered all that you do?

WHAT WILL IT COST?

At the same time as working out what the customers want, you need to work out what it will cost to supply it. If you can also find out what the customers are prepared to pay (what do your rivals charge?), then you have a good indication of the profitability of your business.

Costing is the other side of the operation we look at in the business plan of building up a cash flow projection and profit budget. It goes along with the start-up budget and other figures we look at in the section on raising finance. Between them, they present the full cash profile of the business.

OVERHEADS

Your business will incur two kinds of overheads whatever you intend to supply. First, the **fixed overheads** such as the cost of buying or renting the premises. You must pay these whether or not you sell anything. Then there are the **sales-related** or variable **overheads,** or the cost of supplying each item of goods or service.

It is most important to monitor these once you get going, but you also need to do a bit of intelligent guessing before you start, to make sure you get your pricing right. Costing time can be harder than costing production of, say, a dozen stock items. But it is still calculable.

The starting point is the hourly (or monthly) rate of charge of the member of staff. In your own case, it is how much an hour you intend to make for your efforts. The rate you will have to charge out to customers will need to be higher than this, to take account of non-charged hours, fixed overheads, payroll costs and so on.

For example, Fred is paid £8 an hour for a 40 hour week, plus £12 for overtime. What will be his charge rate, assuming he is attending charged calls for 80 per cent of his time?

Total charged time :

32 hours a week for (say) 47 weeks (allowing for holidays)

= 1504 hours (say 1500).

Total cost of employing Fred (excluding overtime) :

£320 a week plus employer's NI contributions (about 10 per cent) and other direct staff costs of, say, £30 a week, for 52 weeks

= £19,864.

Direct cost per hour :

£19,864 over 1500 hours = £13.24 per hour.

To this we need to add overheads tied up in making Fred's services available. He may have a van permanently at his disposal, plus a full range of spare parts and an extensive tool kit. Then there is the back-up service of accounts, making appointments and so forth. Assume Fred is one of two people employed by the business. The total overhead cost of what they are doing, on an annual basis, is £15,000, allowing for full cost of vans, and all office costs. Fred's share is £7,500

HOW MUCH AN HOUR?

which, spread over his chargeable 1500 hours, means his rate must go up to £18.24 an hour to break even. Your profit margin is to be added to that. Small wonder that so many firms now have call-out fees of £25 or more.

COSTING GOODS

If you are producing goods, work out the cost of each item by reference to the length of charged time you and any staff spend on the item, plus the direct costs of producing it. Again, the profit margin comes on at the end.

If Fred and similarly paid staff were producing items, they would probably be productively employed for more than 32 hours a week (though no doubt less than 40), so the charge rate including all overheads might be, say, £15 an hour. If it takes 4 hours' work to produce one item, using raw materials worth £5, the item costs £65 to produce before allowing for profit, contingencies, and so on.

COST PRICE AND MARKET PRICE

Don't confuse the cost of goods (plus desired profit margin) with the price. What price you can charge depends much less on you than your customers. That is, unless you can get yourself a monopoly for an essential item, which is the privilege only of businesses like the Post Office or specialist firms who are so competitive in their pricing that nobody else can compete with them for their small market.

What the customers want to pay may have little to do with the cost. For example, they may be prepared to pay twice as much for a reliable service than one which delivers the goods erratically. Yet it may cost you only a little extra to gear your firm to guarantee delivery.

Take Fred, for example. His ordinary hourly rate is over £18, but, paradoxically, his hourly charge rate for overtime is less than that. Whilst he gets paid more (and up go the payroll costs), we are recovering all the fixed overhead costs against his ordinary charged hours, so these do not affect overtime hours. But it is a fair bet that customers will more readily pay a higher call-out charge if Fred is prepared to turn out in the evening to sort out their problem than for an ordinary daytime call.

If your pencil has been kept busy you will now have a much better answer to my original question (though it may not be the same one as that with which you started). This is because you can answer some other questions with more confidence: what do the buyers want? Who are they, and why are they buying? What can I supply them with, and what will it cost me to do so?

WHAT WAS IT YOU WERE SELLING?

6   *Raising finance*

*H*OW MUCH MONEY is needed to get started? Where do you get it? We will take the questions in that order, as it is almost as dangerous to raise too much cash as too little.

There are two parts to this:

A budget of how much start-up money is needed, and

A cashflow forecast of how fast cash goes through the business.

A business can founder if it gets either of these wrong, even though it is basically profitable. That is why we need to be careful.

A START-UP BUDGET

Whether you are buying a business, buying into a franchise, or starting from scratch, you need funds to get started. You must buy capital items (the premium on a lease, or new equipment) and cover running costs and your personal expenses until the business becomes profitable. Much of this money is needed at the beginning, with further injections of new money from time to time as things develop.

Below is a checklist of items your start-up budget should cover:

CHECKLIST : START-UP COSTS

Premises

capital cost of buying, or premium and rent in advance	£..........
legal and survey fees	£..........
repair and maintenance	£..........
service charge in advance	£..........
rates due at start	£..........
adaption of premises, eg shop front, telephones	£..........

Plant and machinery

purchase of equipment, or premium under leases	£..........
cost of moving, installing, adapting equipment	£..........
purchase of car or van	£..........
initial running expenses	£..........

Stock

purchase of initial stock for resale, supply	£..........
initial stocks of other consumables, eg leaflets	£..........

Goodwill

if buying a business or franchise, the price	£..........

Staffing

initial wages, commissions, professional fees	£..........
your personal expenses for initial period	£..........

Other

initial interest payments and finance costs	£..........
contingency reserve (to cover what you didn't think about)	£..........

TOTAL (for .... months)   £..........

Have you noticed two hidden variables in this checklist?

The first is that some items can be obtained in different ways - buying or renting premises or equipment; getting cash or credit for stock.

The second is that the timescale can be altered. When do you need cash for personal expenses, and for how long? To tackle the timescale, we need another kind of checklist, a cash flow forecast. This was part of our business plan.

The business should now have three financial plans (or best guesses): a cash flow forecast, a profit forecast and income budget, and a start-up budget. Armed with these, we can see where to start the cash flowing.

RAISING THE CASH

You have two sources of capital: your own, and money granted by or borrowed from others. The relationship between these is regarded as highly significant by professional lenders, and is given a fancy name, **gearing**. The gearing of a business is the ratio:

borrowed capital : own capital

A business is said to be **highly geared** if borrowing is high compared with owner's capital, and low if the reverse holds. Lenders start worrying when a small business is geared more than 1:1. This means that loans exceed assets owned outright, and therefore what the business is worth. Consequently the level of risk is high.

Lenders are concerned to see how much capital the owner is investing. Why should they put their money at risk if you will not? The other point of which they are well aware is that if you invest up to the hilt in your business, you are going to work your hardest to make sure it succeeds. So, the first source of finance must always be **you**.

Probably more than you think. Those who have been made redundant, or have retired, will have some funds available. Do you own your own home? Most of us do. What is it worth? That will depend on where you live. So also will decisions on whether it is wise to sell the house and look for somewhere else cheaper. This will free some cash and, perhaps, cut down on living expenses for the time being. In recent years, the housing market has made some a significant profit, while others have shown large losses. As things pick up in some areas, selling may make sense. In others, it does not. There are no easy rules.

If you don't sell, you may still use your house as security for a mortgage or additional mortgage. This is usually one of the best sources of borrowed money. Don't forget though, that the rest of the family are also living there, so it's their home that's at risk, too. This is something about which you should be completely honest with the family right from the start. When your business proves to be a success, they will enjoy their share of the benefits. But if things do go wrong, perhaps for an unforeseen reason, they will also be at risk.

What about your other savings and investments? These should certainly be used, rather than borrowing more expensively elsewhere. It also helps to keep the gearing in your favour. You may have life assurance policies or small shareholdings that can be cashed in to advantage. However, it may be better to hang on to policies, and to borrow against them instead, at least for the time being. This is for two reasons. First, cashing in a policy early may be a very bad investment decision in its own right. The amount gained may be much smaller than the amount invested, but with a better return in two or three years' time. Also, what may now seem a good idea to save a little, may be bitterly regretted in 20 years' time.

HELP FROM THE FAMILY

Similarly, think through your other assets. Does the family need two cars? Do you know how much a car costs to run each year? My (ordinary estate) car cost over £40 a week last year, while my wife's bang-about Mini cost another £20 a week. Come to that, do you know what your family budget is? How will that fit in with your plans? If you don't know, then your budgeting ought to start **today**, so get that pencil out!

Use the start of your business as the start of your personal economies, not the end of them. It is very tempting to use an expense account or the tax advantages available to get a bigger car. It may seem to have advantages in giving you the right image for your new business - or so any competent car salesman will tell you. But if it bleeds you of badly-needed cash, it will not be long before others are driving the car, and you are at the bus stop.

The family may also help with loans on easy terms - easy, that is, until Uncle Egbert is unexpectedly made redundant and needs his money back urgently. If you borrow that way, it is only fair to realise that they may in future need the capital more than you. What if that happens at a time when it is not easy for you to repay? Be as businesslike with family loans as with loans from strangers.

RAISING CASH
FROM OTHERS

This can be done by getting others to join in your business, or buy a stake in it, or by grants or commercial loans. You can get others involved in the business, and putting up their own capital, in various ways:

By bringing them in as partners, perhaps as **sleeping partners**

By forming a company, and selling them some of the shares

By setting up as a **cooperative**.

The price in each case is that the business is theirs as well as yours. The pros and cons of setting up a company have already been discussed.

GRANTS

There are people prepared to give you money to help your new business get going, if it's the right sort of business in the right place. One of them is me - in my official capacity as one of Her Majesty's payers of tax. There are also business charities willing to help. Why? Enterprise is a good thing, especially in areas of high unemployment.

We look at various sources below in the section about outside help. Check it. There may be help for you that will make quite a difference to your cash projections.

BORROWING FROM
THE BANK

The primary sources of money for the small business are the high street **banks**, all of which have small business units. They can offer help by way of **overdraft** or **fixed term loans**. The cheapest and most flexible method is an overdraft. This means that you can draw up to an agreed amount more out of your bank account than you have in it. You pay interest for this, but on a daily basis and at up to 4 per cent more than the bank's base rate. The idea is that you only pay on what you have borrowed that day. Technically, an overdraft is repayable to the bank on demand. However, if things are not going badly the bank will probably review the overdraft with you each year or so.

One problem with overdrafts and other loans at variable rates is checking how much you actually pay. The calculation of daily rates of interest at constantly changing rates can be hard for non-experts to check. Allegations of overcharging have been made, and sometimes substantiated, so it pays to keep an eye on the total charges. Do not assume that they are always correct.

Fixed interest loans usually cost more, and tie you down more, but are necessary to raise larger amounts of cash. There is plenty of scope for choice at the beginning. This affects the length of the loan, whether there is a **repayment holiday** (a period during which no repayments have to be made) at the beginning of the loan, and so on. But once started, the agreed repayments must be met. And it can be expensive to pay off such loans early.

Plan your borrowing so that you borrow enough (including a margin for error). Always aim to pay it back as soon as practicable - perhaps over a three-year term - unless you can see good profit reasons why longer term loans are necessary.

Lenders like **security** behind a loan. With a company, directors will be asked for personal guarantees. Lenders often also want to see life assurance policies to make sure they get their money back if anything happens to the borrower. They may ask for a mortgage on the owner's or director's house or other assets. But there is help here for you with the government's **Loan Guarantee Scheme**. The government will guarantee up to 70 per cent of your loan, in exchange for a premium from you of £25 for each £1000 borrowed. Ask the bank manager for details.

Besides the banks, others may be prepared to put money up as loans on a commercial basis. Consider, for example **insurance companies**, and also **Investment in Industry** (*3i's*), a company set up by the Bank of England and the major banks specifically to lend money to business. These may be much more interested in larger loans than the clearing banks. If you are confidently thinking big, they may be able to help you think even bigger. The other bodies set up to help small businesses, such as the **Rural Development Commission** (addresses at end) also have access to funds. Sometimes this is at low rates of interest. They may also be able to give grants towards the cost of interest on loans.

To find out about what is available in grants and loans, do not forget to ask your local enterprise agency for help. They will know what's available locally, and might be able to help with introductions. And check with the bank manager whether he knows of other sources.

Don't scout around for loans in a haphazard way. The bank manager will be pleased to see

BE PREPARED

you - if you approach getting the loan in a businesslike way. Do it with the professional attitude to your business you intend to adopt when you get going. Make an appointment, and go armed with some impressive details.

Most important, lenders want to see plans and cash projections. They want to know about your start-up budget, your cashflow projections, your profit and loss budget, and your business plans. If you have not set your pencil to work on these, they will not be very impressed. If you have, they will quite probably help with advice on improving them in addition to coming up with the money, if the figures are right.

A final word. Beware of money that is too easy to come by. Always check the true cost of the loan. Lenders are obliged by law to show you this, as well as a standard form of interest rate - the **APR** or annual percentage rate. Watch for other charges besides the interest, for example setting-up or introduction fees, professional charges and settlement fees at the end. These can add substantially to the total cost of the loan. Watch also that if you borrow through a broker, you can end up paying even more. The **broker's fee** will not be included in the APR. There is another point to watch here. What may happen is that the fee is added to the amount of loan borrowed. It then 'disappears' when granted to leave you with the amount you originally wanted. The result is that you will be paying interest on the charge throughout the period of the loan. That can prove costly.

BUYING ON CREDIT

An alternative means of financing the purchase of cars or equipment is through credit sales or hire purchase. At best these are extremely good ways of buying, but at worst very pricey. I say 'at best' because offers of interest-free credit sales do occur from time to time, allowing you to phase payment over perhaps 10 months on cars and some goods. In other cases the APR may be 30 per cent or more, and much more expensive than borrowing through your bank or on a fixed term loan.

When starting, you may find suppliers will make stock available to you on credit terms or on special sale or return terms. They may also share in special offers with you that cut the cost to you of initial purchases. Franchisers should normally be expected to help their franchisees at the beginning.

Other forms of finance are more readily available for the expanding business and are discussed at the end of the book.

7   *Accounts*

L ET ME INTRODUCE YOU to the black economy. It is frequented by those who keep no books or records of what they do. They never charge VAT nor do they pay NI contributions or income tax. You don't need the introduction, I'm sure. Their approach is simple. It is cheaper for them and cheaper for their customers. If they charge £50, they pocket it. To pocket £50 after income tax, NI and VAT would mean a bill of about £80.

WHO NEEDS ACCOUNTS?

If this tempts you, I could tell you the penalties the tax authorities and the courts impose on such people when they catch them (which they do quite often). But that's not the only reason for keeping things straight. Rather, it is because you need to control your money so that your business grows properly. Earlier in the book, we examined how to set up an initial budget, and how to use a cash-flow budget. If you do not continue to keep accounts, you will have no idea whether your cash-flow follows the projections, or how you are using your money.

One problem is that those in the 'black' economy are often actually in the red. They have no pension to retire on, and no sickness benefit if they are ill. Possibly they also have no savings. And they may have no idea whether they are working for a profit or for nothing. Without good records, you will flounder, and may founder. You will not know how much profit you are making, and will probably lose track of money people owe you (though they won't lose track of your debts). You will not be using the money invested in your business as best you could.

WHAT ACCOUNTS SHOULD I KEEP?

Companies are required to produce accounts annually in a set form, and must keep proper records to satisfy the auditors that the accounts are right. The government is proposing to relax this requirement for the smallest companies. Even after that change, small companies, like partnerships, will need to keep proper books to satisfy the shareholders or partners that they are getting the right share of the profits. A sole trader can keep records in any form he or she likes and these will not need auditing. To give an idea of what a year's accounts should show, some simplified accounts in audited form are shown below, following the format imposed on small companies. Wibble Widgets Ltd is a 100 company, that is, it has 100 £1 shares, 99 of which belong to its director/owner Mr Wibble.

ACCOUNTS OF WIBBLE WIDGETS LTD
Year ending 31 March 19**

Profit and loss account for the year ending 31 March 19**

	£	£
Turnover (sales) :		100000
Cost of sales :(a)		
Opening stock	9000	
Purchases	30000	
Delivery costs	1000	
Wages	30000	
	70000	
less closing stock	10000	
		60000
Gross profit		40000
Rental income		2000
		42000
Less		
Rent and service charge	5000	
Rates	1600	
Heat and light	800	
Telephone	600	
Repairs	1000	
Publicity	400	
Stationery and post	200	
Van expenses	2000	
Insurance	600	
Interest	1000	
Bank charges	200	
Legal and audit fees	400	
Sundries	200	
Depreciation	1000	
Net profit before tax		27000
Tax		3000
Net profit for the year		**24000**

Notes :

(a) The cost of goods sold includes all direct costs of selling the goods. Sometimes this includes wage costs, sometimes not - it is one of the many variable items in accounts. To leave out wage costs here will sharply increase the gross profit, but make no difference to the net profit.

(b) Any unusual features ought to be the subject of notes to the accounts. The law also requires some other points (left out here for simplicity) to be covered in notes.

Balance sheet as at 31 March 19**

ASSETS	£
Fixed assets:	
Land and buildings	12000
Plant and machinery	6000
Fixtures and fittings	2000
Current assets:	
Stock	10000
Debtors	8000
Total	38000

LIABILITIES	
Capital and reserves:	
Share capital paid up	200
Reserves(a)	15800
Creditors :	
Long-term bank loan (b)	10000
Hire purchase	4000
Trade creditors	2000
Bank overdraft	2000
Taxation	3000
Loan to director	1000
Total	38000

Notes :
(a) The reserves include the balance of value of the assets over the other liabilities, as it is the general balance of value of the business. It will equal the reserves of the business at the end of the previous year, plus/minus any changes in the values of the assets plus the net profit for the current year, less the amount of those profits already paid to the owners. The figures suggest that Wibble has already had most of the £24,000 profit.
(b) This is a long-term liability, but the other creditors are all current liabilities as they are repayable at short notice.
(c) The law requires other details, left out for simplicity.

AUDITORS' REPORT TO THE MEMBERS OF WIBBLE WIDGETS LTD
We have audited the above financial statements in accordance with approved Auditing Standards. In our opinion these statements, which were prepared under the historical cost convention, give a true and fair view of the state of the company as at 31 March 19** and its profits for the year ended then and comply with the Companies Acts.

Audit Ors & Co   30 June 19**

The profit and loss account shows the profit (or loss) of the business for a stated period (usually a year). It does so in two stages. First, the gross profit (or direct profit from sales) is shown. This is done by finding the direct cost of sales from the sales receipts, taking account of the amount of stock held at both ends of the period. Then the other administrative costs and overheads are deducted to produce a net profit - the 'bottom line' we so often hear of. Accounts can show us much more than just the profit. We will examine some tests that can be applied later.

Balance sheets are not accounts. They are a sort of 'freeze frame' view of the company on one day - the last of the financial year. It tells us what the business is worth, and how strong it is on that day. A better view can be gained by comparing that picture with those of previous years - again using the tests we shall examine below. What you are doing is using these accounts as management accounts.

KEEPING THE BOOKS

The accounts and balance sheet of a little business like this, while telling a lot, can also be changed significantly, just as can the accounts of any business. For example, wages could have been put as a deduction against gross profits, rather than a figure in finding gross profits. What's the difference? The effect is a decrease in gross profits, but a reduction in the general overheads of the business.

On a balance sheet we do not know how the various items among the assets are valued. How are the (leased) premises worth £12,000, or the van and other equipment £6,000? If the values were to be increased or decreased, the effect would also be to increase or decrease the capital reserves by the same amount. This is because that is the figure which makes the accounts balance.

To keep records necessary to produce accounts and a balance sheet like these Wibble Widgets Ltd needed a full book keeping system. This is also necessary to satisfy the auditors or shareholders that the whole thing has not been invented. What do you need?

The records needed will vary depending on your business. A retailer with a limited range of products sold for cash can get by with the daily till total and a weekly list of expenses, totalling costs and sales up over the year in a simple accounts book, such as those made by Collins. So can a jobbing serviceman who gives out bills, and collects in the cash, for each job as he goes along. The moment sales are for credit, things need tightening (see the next section). And if the owner wants to get some idea of which his best lines are, and how much profit different items make, fuller records are needed. It is wise to design the records so errors can be checked.

Patented paper-based systems requiring double entries (as a fail-safe) such as those sold by Kalamazoo have long been available. The up-to-date equivalent is a simple computer-based system, but exercise books will serve if kept properly. In whatever form, you need:

A **cash book** in which to record all payments and receipts (or total takings)

A **petty cash book** or vouchers to avoid cluttering up the cash book with every packet of biscuits or pencil you buy

Customer accounts (or sales accounts) for all credit sales

Purchase accounts if you want to keep track separately of different kinds of expense, and to check on the bills you owe each supplier and, if you want to keep part of the records confidential,

A **private account** to handle partners' or directors' money.

It is part of an auditor's job to tell you if the books and records are adequate for proper accounting for the business. Even if your business does not need auditing, by far the best people to advise on book keeping are accountants. Ask yours for advice before you make their job harder (and pricier) than it need be.

THE CASH BOOK

This is the heart of the system. It is where you record all business receipts and payments except minor payments noted by a petty cash system. It should record every sum coming into or leaving the business, along with its date, and from whom or to whom it is transferred. In time-honoured conventions, a cash book looks like this:

Receipts				Payments			
date	details	ref	£	date	details	ref	£
29/2	Wangle Widgett	CW1	100 60	29/2	Post Office		16 00
				29/2	Wobble Widgets SW2		62 00

Receipts always go on the left, and payments go on the right. The 'ref' column allows you to insert a reference to another account. For example, the receipt from Wangle Widgets also goes into a customer account CW1.

A petty cash book (or vouchers you can buy in a stationery store) keeps track of the little things every business needs to buy. The simplest way is the little tin box with a cash 'float' replaced by vouchers as it is spent. Each time the float is topped up, the payment is recorded in the cash book.

We use the same format to produce accounts to keep track of transfers between the business and each customer and supplier (or kind of overhead).

SALES AND PURCHASES ACCOUNTS

That will look something similar:

SALES ACCOUNT — Account No:..CWI... Customer..............									
29/1	Invoice 602	10c	00	29/2	CB	Cheque	100	00	

When we supply Wangle Widgets, we enter it into account CW1 on the right-hand side (we have paid them in kind). When they pay, it goes on the left as a receipt, cancelling the other side. It also goes into the cash book as a receipt, showing we now have the money.

Of course, these can be books, cards, a computer programme, forms - even backs of envelopes so long as we don't lose them.

BANK ACCOUNTS

Your bank will also be keeping a parallel set of accounts of all your payments into and out of your bank accounts. These need cross-checking with your own accounts, perhaps every month. Do that for two reasons. The first is to spot any errors made by the bank or any frauds on you and the bank. Secondly, the bank's version of your accounts provides a useful way of spotting your own errors.

To check both the bank's accounts and your own, you should receive monthly statements from the bank, and **reconcile** them with your own accounts. If there are no errors, the balance on the bank statement should be reconciled with the closing balance for the month in your cash book, following this formula :

	Closing bank balance
plus	items not credited
less	cheques unpresented
equals	Closing cash book balance

The **items not credited** are items that have appeared as receipts in your cash book, but have not yet been credited to your bank account. This is perhaps because they have not been paid in. The **cheques unpresented** are those payments which you have sent out, and therefore written into the cash book as paid out, but which have not yet been presented for payment to your bank. As a cheque takes several days to get back to your bank if sent by post, there will normally be some cheques outstanding at the end of any month. If the two totals do not reconcile, start hunting for errors.

SPREADSHEETS

For many people, the easiest way to keep the accounts is now on a computer, using software or programs which are like cash books with built in calculators. Because both the computers themselves and, increasingly, the specialist software, are readily affordable, this may be the best answer. You can either design your own computer-based system using a **spreadsheet** or you can buy a ready-designed one. A spreadsheet is the name of the program that makes your computer screen show a matrix of boxes, into each of which you can put data or information. The magic is that the data can be made to transfer itself simultaneously into other boxes elsewhere. The spreadsheet can also be 'told' to take the information in the box into account in calculations. Spreadsheets vary in complexity, but quite powerful spreadsheet programs now cost under £100. Check, however, that your computer can cope with the required memory.

As an example, if I put £200 into the appropriate box on my cash sheet, the computer can be told to transfer it also to the sales or purchase account (or any other account). Alternatively, it can be sent to a list such as that of sales of particular items, or of particular customers, or of debts outstanding. The computer can also be told to add the £200 into the total of the row and column in which the information is contained (for example, a weekly total) or any other calculation. The most basic form of spreadsheet looks something like this:

	A	B	C	D	E
1					
2					
3					
4				200	
5					
6					

The rows (from A to E) can be named whatever you like, as can the columns (from 1 to 7). You can also have as many as you like, and a grid of any size you like, on most programs. Then you add the figures you want. I have put £200 at D4, and told the computer to add up everything in column D (putting the total in D6) and in row 4 (putting the total in F4).

That could represent, for example, the sale of particular kinds of goods (row 4) on Thursday (column D). From this you can go on to three-dimensional graphing for little extra cost, if that is what you want!

If you do keep your records this way, do not forget to keep a back-up copy of the computer records. For additional safety, keep a hard copy (or print out) as well. If you lose these figures they will be extremely difficult or time-

consuming to replace. It happened last year
when the hard disk on one of our computers
broke down. We were rescued only by the
backup copy on a separate diskette.

Once you have decent accounts, you can see
what you're doing. Your budget will start to
make sense - or nonsense, in which case you
can take action. You can monitor your cash
flow, and act before you hit the rocks. And you
can start to control other people's cash which
ought to be yours. In the next section we look at
controlling credit, and we then discuss managing
through accounts.

MANAGING WITH
FIGURES

8   *Controlling credit*

G IVING CREDIT to customers cannot usually be avoided, but it is risky and costly, because it ties up funds. It should be strictly controlled. Granting credit on any scale is also a tightly regulated business. You must therefore monitor all business credit - to you and by you - fully from the start.

MANAGE CREDIT

Whichever way your customers are granted credit, it is your money involved. It is at risk until you receive it, and cannot be used until then. Further, letting money stand out can be expensive, unless customers are paying properly for the privilege. Yet unpaid bills are a major problem for many small businesses.

Do you need to let customers have credit except for short periods, or at all? Could you insist that your customers pay weekly rather than monthly? Could you allow a discount for those who pay promptly? In reality, those who get the 'discount' pay the proper price. Those who do not get it are paying also for the money you are lending them. Do you pay more promptly than your customers? Do you have to do so? If anything, you should aim to err a little the other way. The trouble is that everyone else is trying that game too. And, in the nature of things, bigger firms get away with it more than smaller businesses. A statement of best practice, **payment on time**, is aimed to encourage prompt payment, and stop businesses being cash-starved by late bills. It is aimed at stopping the practice followed by some large firms of deliberately paying their bills only after a considerable delay.

Several leading businesses have adopted the 'payment on time' code. Yet they still sometimes pay late. Why? It is not usually any fault of senior management in these firms. Rather, budgets within the firms are devolved to local levels, and the local managers are more concerned about their bonuses than your profits. Other firms deliberately follow the policy of paying only when they are made to pay.

Do your customers pay in advance? They should, if you are yourself paying out money for them in advance too. Get a deposit on goods you are ordering, or an advance for buying materials whenever possible. Ask for deposits against work done. That cuts your credit problem. It also gives you protection against customers who want to change their minds. What about budget accounts, savings clubs and similar schemes? You may need to induce customers to use these by special offers, but it can be worth it.

SPEED UP CUSTOMER
PAYMENT

Do not neglect incidental credit. If a customer pays by cheque or credit card, how much **delay**

UNINTENDED CREDIT

is there before you pay it into a bank? Do you pay in daily, or once a week? The whole time that you are holding the cheque your customer is benefiting.

The main source of unintended credit is **inefficiency in billing**. If it takes you a month to make up a bill and your customers have four further weeks to pay, that's two months free credit already. If you do not chase the account promptly, and the customer grudgingly then pays by cheque, another month or more may have gone. You are throughout the time paying for that cash - or your best and promptest customers are. If you have many customers like that, you will be permanently extending thousands of pounds in unnecessary trade credit. This is money you cannot use and for which you are paid nothing.

What steps are you taking to deal with **aged debts**? These are debts that have been unpaid for some time. Separate lists of those bills left unpaid for, say, 30 and 60 days will make sure you devote more time to getting them paid, and are aware of who the slow payers are. Computer-based accounts packages can do that sort of thing automatically. Any other system needs a human equivalent, perhaps a monthly check of all customer accounts.

RETENTIONS

When you finish a job, is it really finished? The sloppy practice of many small businesses under time pressure is to finish enough of the work to get the customer off their back. They then rush off to the next job. The last bits never do get finished, because finding time for them becomes a problem. So, a little embarrassed, you don't send out the bill. Or, more brazenly, you do send the bill, but the customer only pays part of it. If sensible, the customer will keep back quite a bit more than the outstanding work will cost. Your problem is that, if you leave too many ends untied like this, you will run out of cash. You will also create many dissatisfied customers (or, more probably, former customers).

REDUCE THE RISKS

Take steps to ensure that debts from your customers become bad debts as seldom as possible. A bad debt is one you cannot get paid. For example, the debtor has disappeared, or has left the country, or is going bankrupt. Not only are you losing the use of that money, you may never get it. Further, the tax charge on your business is probably based on what you have earned, not what you have received. You may have paid tax on a bad debt before your customer pays it. Only when it becomes clear that your customer will not pay at all will you get tax relief.

Set up a procedure for checking properly, each time a card is used, that the card is valid and that the sales vouchers are filled in correctly. Make sure customers produce a **cheque guarantee card** to back their cheques, and that they are not out of date. Be wary of accepting a company cheque from an unknown customer unless there is, again, some way of confirming it. Many garages, from bitter experience, simply refuse to accept company cheques. Customers can usually pay in some other way, if they can pay at all.

There are, of course, many ways of checking a customer. A little time ago, we bought a car in a small garage. I was utterly amazed when first it was reserved for me without a deposit, and then

I was allowed to drive it away having paid by a cheque that was not cleared or checked in any way. Afterwards, it dawned on me that in chatting while we looked at the car, the garage staff had checked who our family was, and my cheque was taken because they were known. Even so, that assumes that I was who I said I was, and that was not checked.

All that the garage staff needed to do was to pick up the telephone and **ask the bank** whether I was good for the amount of my cheque. Had I been a fraudster, I would probably have disappeared quietly at that point on some pretext. The garage could also have had my cheque **specially cleared** before I was allowed to collect the vehicle. That costs a few pounds, but means prompt payment and early use of the money with the risk gone. As it was, we drove the car around for a week before our bank paid up for us.

Credit cards (Visa and Mastercard are the main international ones) are a two-edged blessing. You get the guarantee of payment, but you have to pay a discount for it. How much will depend both on your business and on the credit card company. And you're not always paid promptly by the charge card company. However, some customers (like me) carry as little cash as possible, so will not buy if you only accept cash. Another advantage to me is that the goods I buy and travel tickets I purchase with my card are backed by insurance. Credit cards are also widely used by businesses to keep tight control on the way that the spending on business expenses of their staff is checked. This also applies to charge cards (such as American Express).

Debit cards such as Switch and Delta are very

different in nature to credit cards. They are, in effect, plastic cheque books. Hence the 'exchequer' advertisements. The amount you charge to the card is set off against my bank balance directly, without credit being involved, just as if I had written you a cheque.

There is considerable fraud in the use of both credit cards and debit cards. However, you are largely protected from it if you take full precautions. Always check the card with the staff on the telephone number provided. Better still, install a small checking machine that does this for you. You can even get portable ones now. And make sure that each card is checked properly. Also make sure you know what to do if a card is being used wrongly.

Check the identity and credit-worthiness of any customer to whom you offer any form of credit on an extensive basis. The following suggestions will help:

TAKE PRECAUTIONS WHEN LENDING

Is he who he says he is? Check banker's cards, driving licences or other evidence of identity, preferably something with a signature or photograph attached. Keep a note of the details of what you checked.

Build in a delay between getting the agreement and delivering the goods, to allow checks to be made.

Ask for references. Inquire where the customer banks, and ask your own bank for a **banker's reference** from the customer's bank. If the person is a student, ask where and check. The reply to a request for a banker's reference will be guarded, but useful. Take up trade references. Do not just think how impressive the reference sounds, and be scared off. You might be calling a bluff.

If you suspect the customer is **bankrupt**, check by searching the official bankruptcy register maintained by the Land Charges Registry. You can get the special forms from any law stationer.

If you suspect the customer has other bad debts, check with the local county court **register of judgment debts**, which lists all debts confirmed as due by the court.

In appropriate cases, employ a **credit reference agency** to check your customer's credit rating. This will check official sources, including also lists of those with hire purchase debts, and probably keep large files of its own. Agencies also have powerful databases to check that the customer is giving you all the right details. For example, is the telephone number right? Is the postcode right? Is the person on the electoral roll at the address given? These and other details can now be checked easily by computer.

If the customer is a **company**, get the files at the Companies Registration Office checked. You can do this cheaply and quickly by a **company search.** This can be used to find out how big the company is, who the directors are, what its address is, and so forth. When dealing with companies, watch the **ultra vires** point dealt with in 'Setting up a Company' If you deal with a company with which you have no connection in good faith, then the law will protect you. It will not let you enforce a company contract if you are on notice that the company has no power under its objects to make that contract.

Get **security** for your loan - big business does. If dealing with a company, get a guarantee from the directors. If dealing with a young person for the first time, get a security deposit or a personal guarantee from someone else (the gas and electricity people do just this). Or make sure you protect your **seller's lien** (the right of an unpaid seller to hold the goods), or **reserve the title** in the goods until you are paid, by using properly drawn up standard conditions (see 'Big sales, small print') and get legal advice.

Make it clear you **get tough** on defaulting debtors. Check out the best way of getting a debt enforced, and let it be known that you will use that route

ENFORCING PAYMENT

Inevitably, someone will default on you. Take proper precautions to reduce and check credit, and you may avoid the problem in part, but it will come. When it happens, you need a procedure to deal with it. Start with an aged debtors procedure. Send a clear reminder after, say, 30 days, and a stronger one after another 15 or 30. After that, you could telephone to find out why payment is not made, having first decided what you regard as a plausible excuse, if any! At this point, check any contract you have. Are you entitled to seize the goods back, or demand an arbitration?

If all else fails to get the bill paid, either take firm

action, or write the bill off there and then. Do not waste time sending endless reminders if you propose to do nothing further. It should be said immediately that taking court action may not be worthwhile to cover a smaller bill if you get your solicitor to do it. And by 'smaller' I mean less than about £200. You can however collect these yourself through the County Court's **Small Claims** procedure. Your local county court has a booklet on *Small claims* that explains it, and the court clerks will also help.

Even a solicitor's letter costs money. But a firm letter threatening proceedings in a formal manner, and giving a short period of 7 to 14 days, addressed to a senior member of the business gets many bills paid. It is worth sending letters of this sort by recorded delivery postal services. That way you can prove that the formal demand of payment was received by the debtor. After that, court proceedings are your only course of action. Two points may be emphasised on this. First, proceedings through the small claims side of the county court are now fairly efficient and reasonably cost effective. The legalese and procedures have been cut back to a minimum. Second, court proceedings can be slow. Further, always remember that there is no guarantee that the judgment you obtain will be paid. If the debtor is unemployed, or has no assets, you are wasting your time. That should also be checked if possible first.

BANKRUPTCY AND LIQUIDATION

When a business runs out of money, there is usually something left. This goes first to any secured creditors - that is, those with mortgages, seller's liens, and similar arrangements. Next come the employees and the government (to collect taxes outstanding). Only then come the ordinary trade creditors. Sometimes there will be some money for them, but not much. In such cases, the liquidator pays a 'dividend' to each of the creditors who has registered as being owed money by the bankrupt. It is only part payment, but make sure you register any claim. When the bankruptcy has become official, you may get tax relief if you had previously paid tax on the money you will not now receive.

Making a debtor bankrupt is the last resort of a creditor. It is expensive and, for the reasons just shown, does not always work. But it is an extremely powerful threat as it may result in the debtor losing his or her home and possibly job. Any bank accounts, savings and most other assets will also be seized. Get legal advice before you take such a drastic and expensive step.

All those lending money to consumers as part of their business, or advising on credit, need to have a consumer credit licence. There are various kinds of licence depending on what you are doing. The Office of Fair Trading publishes a series of booklets about this. Your local library or TEC (Training and Enterprise Council) can probably help you get them. Make enquiries at the start if your business involves the grant of, or advice about, credit. This does not include the ordinary credit where customers are given a short period to pay.

CONSUMER CREDIT
LICENCES

9   *What accounts can tell you*

A SET OF ACCOUNTS tells you far more about the business than whether it is making a profit. Accounts tell you how and where that profit is being made. Seemingly innocent figures can reveal both strengths and weaknesses, particularly if you can compare a series of years. Take one year in isolation. With a bit of creative accounting, some hard work, and an extra effort to increase turnover and collect overdue bills combined with a slowness in paying bills out, a competent bookkeeper can work a few miracles. It will not be kept up.

There is a full set of accounts in the section on 'Controlling your credit'. As an exercise, try the following tests out on those accounts. What conclusions should you draw if Wibble Widgets were your firm?

FINANCIAL SOUNDNESS

The most fundamental aspect of the financial soundness of a business is the level of its borrowings compared with its total financial strength. If you are thinking of expanding, or of buying another business, you need to know how sound the business is. Watch the **current ratio**. Anyone from whom you seek to borrow will do so. This is the ratio:

current assets : current liabilities

Both these figures are found on the balance sheet. What the ratio shows is how readily the business can pay its current debts. If the figures are near to or less than 1:1, then there are signs of potential trouble.

What if you suddenly had to pay all the debts (eg the overdraft was called in)? Could you sell all the stock at its balance sheet valuation? Probably not. For this reason, there is an even tighter ratio to watch, the liquidity ratio or **acid test**. This is:

current assets less stock: current liabilities

In other words, forgetting about the stock, how much money is there to meet all current creditors? If that ratio is strongly adverse, where does the money come from to meet the money owing to the creditors if they start pushing for payment?

A low ratio may suggest that there is too much short-term credit in the business. A high ratio suggests that there is a good reserve of long-term credit or owner's capital. Looked at another way, a low ratio may mean that the owners have been taking money out of the business, rather than letting it build up. Check the ratios for previous years. Are they better or worse? If they are getting worse, are you taking the right decisions about investment? Two useful credit ratios may show you what is happening.

The two ratios are:

CREDIT RATIOS

    creditors : purchases
    and
    debts : credit sales

What are these telling us? They are both measures of the efficiency of the business in getting its debts settled. The point behind the ratios is usually made clearer by presenting the figures in a way that shows how many days the average debt or credit is outstanding.

Say that the creditors' figure is £5,000 and the total purchases are £50,000. That gives a rather meaningless ratio of 1:10. Now, multiply the first figure by 365 (or 52 if you want weeks), and then divide it by the second figure. That gives a figure of 36 days or 5 weeks. This means the business is taking 5 weeks on average to pay its bills. If creditors are usually extending 30 days net terms, that is not so bad. If their terms are 14 or 7 days, then things have clearly been allowed to slip.

Take the debts ratio. Say the figures are £20,000 on total sales of £75,000, or 1:3.75. On a daily basis, this is about 97 days or 14 weeks. Something may be badly wrong here. Whether or not it is bad will depend on the business. What would spell bankruptcy for a greengrocer would be a miracle in selling an aircraft. But it may be that not all the customers are that slow in paying - rather, the figure hides some bad debts that are unlikely to be paid.

This suggests that these need identifying.

Here again, trends are useful. How have these two ratios changed from one year to another? If they are very healthy, there may be scope for changing them in your favour by speeding up the collection of the debts and slowing down the rate of paying creditors. A colleague of mine took an extra one million pounds in for his business in one year just by doing that. Nor did it really affect the business's relationships with its customers or suppliers. But it can be worked the other way, if your suppliers suddenly tighten up on their terms, and you are relying too heavily on their credit.

Other standard tests applied to businesses are those showing its **gross profit ratio** and **net profit ratio.** The gross profit ratio is the proportion of gross profits to total sales. This reflects the mark-up or margin on sales of goods averaged out across the whole business.
It is calculated simply by taking the ratio:

BUSINESS EFFICIENCY

$$\frac{\textbf{gross profit x 100}}{\textbf{total sales}} = \textbf{gross profit \%}$$

The net profit ratio is the net profit after taking out all costs as a proportion of total sales, in the same way. The percentages do not mean very much on their own. Again, trends are all-important. Is the business becoming more or less profitable? If so, why? Have a look at individual overheads in the same way. In many businesses the local rates have been rising fast in recent years. Have profits kept pace? How do the figures compare with the usual profit ratios for that kind of business, or the national averages? To find this out, see below.

If your business is selling goods, particularly retail sales, other figures can help here in showing the real throughput of stock in the business. There are two measures to look for, again from the accounts. The first is the figure for sales per square metre of the shop or store. For this you compare the sales figures for a given period with the area of the showroom or shop. Another figure is the 'shelf life' of the stock. This can be judged by finding out how many times the stock is turned over in a year. Compare the opening and closing balances of stock with the total throughput of stock during the year.

For example, these figures may show that the stock is on average turned over ten times a year. Whether that is good or bad will very much depend on the type of business. It also depends on whether the business is carrying a relatively high or relatively low level of stock. Read that with the rental costs, and we get some idea of 'shelf rent', the amount it costs us to store stock between purchase and sale. If our stock is turning over ten times a year, it is costing about ten per cent of the annual rent, rates, etc, to store the stock between purchase and sale.

In most retail businesses, a reasonable level of stock must be carried to attract the customer. For an antique shop or car sales business, there is little that can be done about this. Much has, however, been done in other businesses to minimise shelf rent. It can be done by cutting to a minimum the rental and other costs of the space used, by using out of town sites. Or the turnover of stock can be monitored to give precise knowledge of sales. The bar-coding of goods enables any till equipped with a laser reader and the necessary electronic equipment to read and record the details of all stock sold. The same information gathered on the age-old methods of lists will also serve to break down the profits figures between different kinds of goods or services.

In a manufacturing or service business, it may be possible to reduce the stock levels almost to zero. As we have discussed in connection with business plans, adopting the 'just in time' approach to stock buying may mean we have no stock rent to pay at all. Lax stock control may be tying up large amounts of cash.

A final figure to watch for is the return on owner's capital. Owner's capital is the amount of money invested in the business by its owners. For example, it may be used in buying the business, or in capital costs of buildings, equipment and initial stock. Find the ratio :

net profits : owner's capital

and you really find out whether your money might not be better left in a deposit account! For example, if our business is tying up £30,000 in owner's capital, and the net profit is £12,000, the return is 40 per cent. This is not so bad. However, if we put the money in the bank we would make perhaps £1,500 or more in any event. This leaves £10,000 to pay us for our efforts. How much effort is it?

Armed with these figures, we have some idea of the real shape of the business. Better still, we should compare it with similar businesses. This is how tax officials check on who is and who is not fiddling their accounts. They work out the gross and net profits (and other ratios) for all the businesses of a particular kind in an area. Say that all the local fish and chip shops are making a gross profit of 35 per cent. It is a fair bet that if they find an owner who claims only to be making a profit of 15 per cent in a shop that clearly is doing a fair trade they will suspect he is on the fiddle.

Usefully to you, the Revenue publish these figures as their *Business Economic Notes* on a national basis. The Government's *Business Monitors* for each sector of industry also give a national picture of the profitability of a business, and other information may be available through local libraries. Beyond that, you are going to need to consult appropriate experts who can advise you about the business from their own local experience.

10 *Publicity*

YOUR PRODUCT IS very good value for money. It is an excellent product, and you are a person with whom any sensible customer will want to do business. This is because you know what your customers want, and you know you can supply it the way they want it. You can do this at a price they also like. You have done your market research and your product planning, and you know that these statements are true.

Do the customers know that? Probably not, so - go tell them. Tell as many of them as you can. After all, you are doing them a favour. How do you best do that?

A CHECKLIST FOR SUCCESS

First, there is another job for your pencil. Get a sheet of paper, and write on it all possible advantages customers can gain from your product. You want to list all the answers you can think of to this question:

My customers will want to buy this because ...

....

....

....

....

....

....

....

....

Engage in a bit of brain-storming. Write down everything that comes to mind, however daft it might sound. Even better, get one or two others to help you do this, so you feed off each others' ideas. If you find your list is a little short, perhaps a bit more product planning is called for, so that you can say, for example, 'It looks good'. Add to the list all the facilities that go with your product - pleasant service, prompt delivery, out-of-hours repair service. Look at every aspect of what you are selling and how you are selling it.

If you run out of ideas, find how others are selling similar products. How do they let everyone know how good they are? You should already know, because in your market research you should have accumulated details of all your rivals' products. If you have not, it is still not too late!

When your list is complete, you have your checklist for success. Somewhere in this list is what your customers want to hear, and the best reason for buying from you. I must add a word of warning. Keep the list completely honest. Do not try to fool anyone. You want your customers to stay good customers. If your product is not worth having, it needs changing. Do not pretend that advertising will solve all your problems. Change the product, or its price.

Now write a much shorter list. Put in this list only the best reasons for buying from you. What you are after are your **unique selling points**, even if there is only one. Your USPs are the points about your product that you can offer, but no one else can, to your customers. That brings us to the next list.

THE WANTED PERSONS LIST

Who will buy? Hold on! That's not a new question. No - but we now need the answer. In reality, the whole world will not want to buy, though they may all need telling, so your customers hear your message. Somewhere out there are *your* customers, and you now need to write down as clearly as you can who they are. The more specific your description, the better. Just like the police, until you have a good description, you don't stand so much chance of catching those you are after.

HOW TO SPREAD THE GOOD NEWS

We now have the ammunition and the target. How do we hit that bull's eye? In advertising, as on a shooting range, there are many ways of doing this. There can be the long-distance telescopic rifle with night sights, the machine gun, or even the anti-tank missile. Or, if you like, there can be the hard-sell salesman, the newspaper advertisement, or the sort of splurge we get from politicians at election time. All work well on the right customers.

Which are the weapons for you? Forget television; it costs far too much. Similarly, forget the national newspapers full-page ads. Your publicity budget does not allow you to think that big, though those forms of advertisement can be extremely effective. So can much more modest local advertising. Here are some more realistic alternatives:

Local newspapers - both the weeklies and, increasingly, the free local papers. They, in particular, live by advertising so will be only too keen to help you advertise through them.

Small ads in national papers, particularly at the weekends or in specialist features. Similarly ads in the specialist journals for your trade will help. There's a complete guide to this sort of advertising, called **British Rate and Data.** Check it in your local library. It tells you the key details, including cost and the circulation.

Local radio - if your message should be heard not read, what better?

Direct mail - post your message as a letter or leaflet to everyone you can find who fits your 'wanted person' description. This is said to be the most effective form of advertising, **providing** you have the right mailing list. That you can get from those same directories we discussed in the section on market research - or telephone directories. If you want a complete list of everyone in a certain area, get the electoral register from the local council.

Telephone sales - this can also be targeted, and is increasingly used as a sales technique on 'cold' calls, those with no previous contact. This is a widespread method, and it works well, although it can also cause considerable irritation. I was, I must say, extremely rude to a telephone sales person who chose to telephone while I was watching the closing minutes of the Cup Final on television!

You are selling this way every time anyone phones. Are you always busy? Do you have one of those bored, rude telephonists? Or can you charm them over the wires?

Posters - I'm one of millions who spend their lives staring at posters on stations, underground trains, buses, taxis, walls .... They work, don't they? Your display does not have to be as elaborate as many of those. But if your shop is at one end of a shopping street, should not something at the other end of the street tell your customers where you are?

Leaflets - you can give these out several ways, by standing in the street, putting them through letter boxes, advertising that people who write in will get one, putting them in the shops, inserting them in local newspapers or specialist journals, or getting them delivered by the newsagent with the local papers. All these methods are in constant use. Like direct mail, the technique works if the leaflet is designed well. The best are the useful little ones people keep for future reference.

Point of sale displays - make sure the product is well presented where it is going to sell, with support from posters, leaflets, or a well-designed display. If you are retailing, your whole shop-front is a big advertisement of your products and you. If it is dowdy and untidy, can the customers expect better of you? Why not provide lots of advertising space for your suppliers to sell their, and your, wares.

Packaging - the advertising that personally most annoys me is that which stares at me from the cereal packets every breakfast time.

The children love them, and regularly fight over who can read which. How much free advertising space is provided by you in your house or office? Is your product one that should be packaged well so that it gets its place in this free display?

Direct selling - somehow, Britain has a history of sneering at its salesmen. Why? I do not know. One success of recent governments has been to make us less inclined to sneer, and more inclined to imitate. If we don't, someone else will. If you can't, you need to get someone who can, whether behind the shop counter or on the doorstep. You need people who can get on well with others and size up their customers accurately. Don't forget to make sure they know exactly why your products are worth buying - and worth them selling.

Make your product into news - perhaps the most effective advertising of all is on News at Ten. Think what those shocking famine films wrung from us all in relief aid. That's the extreme case, but think how many others get their products or themselves free advertising by being news. It takes a bit of flair, and someone who does not mind the publicity, but if you can just be different, then you can be news. After all, local journalists have a great deal of space to fill each week. Even better if what you do has a photograph or two attached - that fills space even faster. Give it a human touch. The best stories always quote someone saying something. If you send something off to the newspapers, don't forget the quote. Better still if you are going to be a good advertiser. They owe you a favour!

That's at least ten ways of going about it. Which you choose will depend on your product. If you are running a taxi, make sure you advertise in the phone book, while a national advertisement might be a crazy waste of money. Is that true of selling package holidays? Whichever way you choose, you also need good copy, that is, wording, design and pictures in your advertising.

HIT 'EM HARD!

Now your pencil must really go to work. You have to work out your sales message. Remember, you now know at exactly whom your advertisement is aimed, and exactly what it is that they will find best about your product. So, tell them in good, clear, plain English. Make the message attractive, like the product. Choose good, honest headlines. Look at the way the experts advertise to your sort of customer. Think pictures as well. Just as photos liven up the news in the papers, so do cartoons, photos, and logos in the ads.

Most home computers now have powerful graphics programs on them. They also have desk top publishing (DTP) programs. These are now becoming standard in the software packages that are sold with PCs. Using them, you can design and try out many forms of leaflet, poster or advertisement. They will help you with logos and letterheads. In particular, you can try things out in several ways and print styles until you are happy with the result. In this area, the computer has become mightier than the pencil! If you have a printer that can print the graphics the computer generates, you can, if you wish, do the entire thing yourself.

If your pencil and your computer both fail you, get outside help. Advertising agents will help you shape up your campaign, advise you on how and where to advertise, and place those advertisements or prepare and print those leaflets for you. They'll charge, but perhaps not as much as you think, because they get commission from those selling advertising as well. The advertising staff at the local paper can give guidance on effective use of their paper, as will the local printers.

GET YOUR IMAGE RIGHT

Whatever you do is part of your advertising. Make sure the 'incidental advertising' gives the right message as well. This covers everything from your stationery to, for example, your waiting room. Have you had to sit for ages on a wooden bench in a doctor's waiting room with only a year-old copy of *Country Life* to keep you company? If the doctor cares that little about his patients while they wait to see him, is he going to care when examining them? Does your waiting area impress or depress?

Finally, do not neglect your business name and image. Choose and stick to an identity, perhaps backed by a logo or a particular colour you always use for your name. Get something that your customers are going to identify as 'you'. Traditionally, people were proud to call their businesses by their own names. Would it really pay a solicitors' firm to be called Doolittle & Dally? Indeed, some solicitors have even dropped that name as old-fashioned. They are 'business lawyers ' these days.

While referring to the law, you should be aware of the laws behind selling, which we look at in the next section.

11   *Big sales, small prin*

*O*PPOSITE IS AN INVOICE received from Shark Supplies for some emergency parts provided for you yesterday. The bill is for more than twice as much as you thought (even before adding the extras). What is more some of the parts didn't work. It cost you another £100 to get the things fitted properly when Dolphin Services put things right this morning. Do you have to pay?

'your problem is our opportunity

Shark Supplies

Unit 10, Waterway Estate
Crabington, Bucks MK92 1Q2

Phone: 0654 321090 (Voice) 0654 321191 (Fax)   VAT No. 0654 3210 98
Emergencies: 0901 234564

All Supplies on our standard terms and conditions (see over)

INVOICE dated....30/2.......1994

30 Feb

To supplying and fitting
replacement placer
widget on customer's
promises, as per
urgent order   300

urgent order supplement   100
parts   50
delivery   50   500.00

Plus VAT at 17.5%   87.50
Due   £587.50

1 Did you remember to look at the small print on the back of the invoice. Most people don't. Which is, of course, why sellers and buyers alike both resort to it in order to stack the contract terms of the sale on the invoice as much in their own interests and against those of the other party to the contract as they can, whilst no one else is looking. The other purpose of the small print is to clear up all the legal doubts and unstated terms of the usual business contract. The rest of the small print on this page looks at issues that could have been hidden in the small print - along with those which the law imposes or forbids.

2 Standard terms The terms and conditions set out herein (hereinafter referred to as the 'standard terms') form part of the terms and conditions of the sale of goods and supply of services invoiced on this document. The buyer agrees to them by signing the document. The seller's servants and agents have no authority to alter them by any oral representation, and the terms can only be altered by express written alteration properly authorised by the seller.

3 Quotations and estimates The price payable by the buyer for goods and services supplied by the seller is that shown on this invoice notwithstanding any quotation or estimate or other sum quoted or estimated by the seller to the buyer at any time. Any such quotation or estimate whilst being given in good faith is to be taken as a rough guide price only, exclusive of value added tax, and exclusive of the seller's standard additional charges for immediate and urgent work, for delivery, and any other additions by the seller according to the standard tariff charges of the seller as published for the time being. Any extra goods or services ordered by the customer are chargeable to the customer in full.

4 Goods and services to be supplied Whilst the seller will use its best endeavours to ensure that the goods supplied by it are fully to the buyer's specifications (or in the absence of specifications are of a reasonable quality for the work to be undertaken by the seller) and that the services supplied by the seller are of a reasonable quality the seller undertakes no warranty whatsoever as to the quality of goods and services supplied and the buyer is on notice to raise with the seller's appropriate representative before the supply of goods is accepted or before any supply of services is completed and for the purposes of this provision a supply of goods is treated as taking place when the goods are appropriated to the buyer's order whether or not they have been delivered to the buyer at that time and a supply of services is taken to be completed at the time stated by the seller's representatives to be the completion of the work. The Sale of Goods Act shall not apply to this contract.

5 Terms of payment Payment of this invoice is due seven days from the date thereof whether or not it has been delivered to the buyer within that time, and the seller shall have the right to charge interest at ten per cent above the basic lending rate of its banker as posted by that banker from time to time on any moneys outstanding from the date that payment on the invoice is due. Payment by instalments or retentions against work are not acceptable to the seller unless agreed in advance of the work being undertaken or the goods delivered.

6 Seller's lien The seller retains the title to all goods supplied until such time as the buyer has paid in full the sums owed to the seller as invoiced by the seller for goods and services supplied. In the event of non-payment of all charges so invoiced the seller reserves in full its rights to the property in all goods supplied including the right to enter upon the buyer's premises at any time of day or night to repossess the goods provided only that the seller in removing the goods shall not cause more damage to the buyer's premises and equipment than is reasonable in removing the goods as aforesaid.

7 Delivery Unless the seller and buyer agree otherwise before the conclusion of the contract for supply evidenced by this invoice the buyer shall be at risk in respect of all goods to be supplied from the time that they are unconditionally assigned to the buyer by the seller or at the seller's order. Whilst the seller will normally arrange for the delivery of goods the seller shall be entitled to charge the buyer for this delivery. Further the seller accepts no responsibility whatsoever for any delay occasioned in the delivery of goods or in the supply of services or any consequent damage that may be occasioned to the buyer or any other person by reason of the delay.

8 Disputes In the event of the buyer raising any issue under this contract or disputing in any way the correctness of the price, delivery, quality, quantity, or any other aspect of the goods or services supplied under this contract the buyer shall not be permitted to take any action in the courts and the seller reserves the right to refer the matter in the absence of agreement to an arbitrator selected by the seller and the buyer shall bear the costs of all fees payable to the arbitrator in respect of such arbitration provided only that such charges shall be reasonable for the work undertaken on the seller's instructions.

9 General And if you thought these terms and conditions were splendid and just what you ought to put in your contract - don't, because you might well be committing a criminal offence, and even if it was not criminal several of these terms will not work in law and anyway they are appallingly written even for legal English.

This pretend small print was designed to bring out two points. The first is to sort out when a **contract** is reached for a supply. The second is to emphasise the importance of the **laws governing sales**, especially consumer sales.

WHEN AGREEMENT IS REACHED

The law requires three things (in England - Scottish law is different and should be checked) before accepting that people are legally bound by a contract. There must be an **offer** by someone to do something. That offer must be **accepted** by someone else, and there must be **consideration** given by one party to the other, that is, money or something else of value changes hands. In practice, these things are not problems, but what is a problem is deciding when the contract is made, and what terms are part of it.

A contract is made at the time the offer is accepted, and on the terms then applying. Suppose Shark Supplies had used their 'standard terms' on an invoice sent as a quotation, or offer, by them. You accept, but do so on a similar standard letter, referring to your own standard terms. In that case your letter is the acceptance and your standards terms apply to the contract, not Shark's. If it was you that sent the first letter, and Shark that accepted, then Shark's terms apply. This is what is called the 'battle of the forms'. It pays to watch it.

SELLING AND THE LAW

Traditionally, the law of sale was quite simple: *caveat emptor* or, let the buyer beware. The terms were whatever the two parties agreed. Put another way, the big fishes were allowed to eat the little fishes. The Shark Supplies approach was the winning approach. The small consumer was the loser.

The law has stepped in with a series of important Acts:

The Sale of Goods Acts and the Supply of Goods and Services Act,

The Trades Descriptions Acts,

The Fair Trading Act,

The Consumer Protection Acts,

The Weights and Measures Acts,

The Consumer Safety Acts,

The Consumer Credit Act

The list is long. Many of these Acts deal with all sales and supplies. Others cover only supplies to private consumers. Further, now we are in the Single European Market, you are required to comply with any relevant European laws. In practice, the British rules have been altered to match the European requirements. The result is a standard set of laws on, for example, labelling, that applies throughout Western Europe. Let's see what effect all these rules have on Shark Supplies' terms.

Clause 2 is a good example of the problems of handling small print. Part of it is rubbish. You only deal on Shark's terms if they form part of the acceptance by Shark of your offer, or you accept Shark's offer with these terms in it and without objecting. Even then they only form part of the agreement if drawn to your attention. Here, Shark would say they were, because it said (see conditions over) on the front of the form. Merely signing the form is not important, and the wording on the form cannot change this. The other part of the wording is notice that limits the authority of all Shark staff to alter these terms. If you reached a verbal agreement with a Shark salesman that altered one of the terms, Shark could say it was not authorised, and go back to their standard terms. Again, whether this is effective will depend on more than this tiny wording.

The clauses on quotes, payment and deliveries are important, but again Shark Supplies is trying it on. The price is - or should be - agreed when the contract is made. If a price has not been agreed, it is quite possible that there is no real agreement, and therefore no contract. Once it is fixed, or its basis is agreed, that cannot be changed. It's no good going back and saying a mistake was made, or that a standard charge not yet mentioned is 'always added' to bills. For the same reason, if you do not mention VAT, and then add it on, the customer would be fully entitled to refuse to pay. If VAT is not mentioned, it is assumed to be included in the price. Further, under the Consumer Protection Act it is an offence to give any consumer a misleading indication of goods, service, accommodation or facilities. Shark might fall foul of that, as well as the Trades Descriptions Acts.

The clause on the quality of goods and services is also illegal. All contracts to consumers, whether formal, or over the counter sales, must contain these terms:

Goods must **correspond with their description**. If they don't, consumers must be entitled to a refund, or to goods that do match the description, and possibly to compensation.

Goods sold by sample must **match the sample**. Again, if they don't, the customer can demand his money back.

Goods must be **fit for the purpose** for which they are supplied. If Shark was asked for parts for a particular purpose, they must work for that purpose.

Goods sold by description must be of **merchantable quality**, unless the seller has pointed out defects to the buyer, the buyer has inspected or has been given a chance to inspect. This means, in effect, they must be reasonable value for the price paid. Sale goods, even if there is no inspection, will not be expected to be as good as full price goods.

THE BUYER'S REMEDIES

These terms apply whatever the contract says. It is an offence to try, as Shark does, to get out of them. Do not, therefore, attempt to use wording of this nature. It is against the criminal law, and the civil courts will not enforce it either. If you want further guidance, get in touch with your local council's **Trading Standards officers**, whose job it is to supervise these laws, and who are as ready to advise retailers as consumers.

The clause trying to remove the buyer's right to a remedy also will not work. But the law is confusing. For example, the following is illegal:

NO REFUNDS MADE AFTER PURCHASE

while there is nothing wrong with this:

NO GOODS EXCHANGED AFTER PURCHASE

Why? Because a seller is never required to exchange goods, faulty or not. His obligation in law is:

either to refund money if the goods are not what is ordered under the contract, and the buyer returns the goods for that reason within a reasonable time, or to pay damages (or compensation) if the goods fall short of the required standard and the buyer chooses to keep them.

Attempting to avoid a customer's right to a refund in appropriate cases is illegal. Refusing to exchange goods - even faulty goods - is not. The law is of course way out of line with what most people want and shopkeepers in particular need both to comply with their customers' wishes and the law.

Though the law deals with all those points, it does not deal, for instance, with delivery nor the seller's lien (which Shark is not alone in claiming). A proper contract should cover all these points. In a more sensible way than Shark's terms, it may cover arbitration too. Many trade associations (for example, travel agents and removers) have standard conditions worked out for the association. Some businesses have standard agreed forms of contract (especially in building and engineering). Get hold of these, and check if they are appropriate. Especially if you are in an unusual business, or there are higher than usual risks of disputes, get a lawyer to assess the problems and advise you on any standard conditions.

USE PROPER STANDARD CONDITIONS

12   *Location*

*T*WO CRUCIAL DECISIONS you will make - possibly by doing nothing - are the location of your business and the kind of premises you base it in. This section aims to alert you to thinking about advantages and disadvantages of different locations and buildings.

MOVING TO THE BEST AREA

What is 'best' varies enormously between businesses. It is not always where you now are. Some businesses have flexibility of location. For them, economic and financial factors can combine to make some areas more attractive locations because of lower overheads and local financial aid. Modern communications have helped this flexibility.

LOCAL OVERHEADS

The cost of business premises ranges widely around the country. Land and rental prices vary between city and country, and between different parts of the country. In rural areas, and some depressed urban areas you may get a new factory or even an office rent-free for an initial period. This variation in cost is reinforced at present by the local operation of the national business rate. Although the rate has now been standardised nationally, the burden depends on the value of each property. These are still higher in city centres than in rural areas.

Other overheads also vary, such as labour costs. These are at their highest in the London travel-to-work area (which extends as far as Oxford), though employees may be better off elsewhere because of cheaper housing. Services cost more in that area, too.

For a retail business, and for some services, this will be perhaps the most critical part of your planning. It's no good opening up where nobody can find you, or where the double yellow lines (painted by the council just after you arrived) stop all parking. It is time for pencil and paper again. Work out what you are looking for before you go hunting. Don't allow yourself to be persuaded something is ideal when it will not do. Some points to consider :

MOVING TO THE
RIGHT PREMISES

What premises do you need - workshop, office, store, shop, garage, other?

How big should they be?

Where should they be - high street, side street, ground level, upstairs, doesn't matter?

Do all the premises have to be together?

What extra facilities will your business

need?

How important is appearance - to customers, to your employees, to you?

What should it cost - rent or mortgage, rates, service charges, running costs, alterations, repairs?

GOVERNMENT AND
LOCAL AID

Financial help and advice is available for small businesses from government and local councils and some private sources to encourage or protect businesses in specified areas. Contact the local councils for the full story for your area. The following lists key kinds of support available.

By special tax reliefs :
Businesses based in an **Enterprise Zone** pay no rates for several years and get full capital allowances for tax purposes on business building costs. This means that the full cost of new buildings can be set against corporation or income tax. There are 25 EZs, usually in city centres or areas of de-industrialisation. They have other advantages, such as relaxed planning procedures, and exemption from industrial training levies.

Import and export businesses may find some help from organising their transportation through a **Freeport,** providing postponement of customs duty and VAT until goods leave the freeport, plus relaxation of some formalities.

The only offset otherwise available

against tax are grants paid in **Northern Ireland** only to offset the cost of corporation tax on certain projects.

By grants :

Smaller businesses setting up in or moving to an **Assisted Area** are entitled to seek capital grants from the DTI. Other grants are paid as **Regional Selective Assistance** in both the assisted areas, and additional **Intermediate Areas**, by way of project grants and training grants. These help projects designed to increase or protect employment in the area. These grants are administered by the **Regional Development Grant Offices** of the DTI (Department of Trade and Industry). Separate schemes apply in Scotland, Wales and Northern Ireland.

Local authorities have powers to help small businesses get established in their areas, though they deviate widely as to how they do this. One programme aims at helping the **Inner Urban Areas**, and funds are available for inner city developments. More generally, councils can give valuable advice, backed in some cases by material assistance in the form of grants, loans or, sometimes, low-cost factory units or help with housing. Some councils devote their attention to making sure you know they are (or think they are) at the centre of things - but seem to have spent all their budget on advertising when you ask for help. Others do less advertising, but provide solid advice when you find them. Ask around.

AID FROM LOCAL
COUNCILS

GET PERMISSION

Wherever you choose to go, make sure you have permission for what you intend to do. No new building can be erected or other works started, and no existing building can be used in a materially different way from its present use, without **planning permission** from the local council. Local councils use planning permission to prevent people using land in ways the council does not want, so you will find limits on where you can start your business. In practice, you can use land for the same broad range of uses as its current use (provided, of course, that is legal). So, a shop can be used for selling most kinds of goods without extra planning permission.

You may also need the permission of the landowner, if you are a tenant. Even if you own the land, it may be subject to **restrictive covenants** which may prevent you using the land the way you want to. These are limits placed on uses of freehold land by a previous owner. If worried, your solicitor will advise.

New buildings - and alterations - must comply with the **building regulations** supervised by the local council. Architects and builders should take these into account in any work they do, but plans will need to be sent to the local council for approval, in addition to any plans needed for planning permission.

BUY OR RENT?

While ideally it is best in the long term to own most premises as an investment, this may prove too costly. It may tie you down too tightly. Or it may be impossible to buy because no freehold premises are available, and you will need to rent. When renting, the crucial points are - how much, and for how long?

The cost can come in several ways :

> a premium or lump sum for the right to buy the lease;

> rent on a regular basis, and which will no doubt increase from time to time (watch when the next rent review is due);

> service charges for landlord's maintenance and other costs (watch how that is worked out);

> VAT (value added tax is added to the rent of some premises, and is also added to the service charges); and stamp duty (which applies to the lease agreement).

The time bought may be just a week at a time, or a fixed period of several years - check this. Which is best in your interests?

If renting, watch two sets of rules. One set usually works for you, and the other usually against you. The set working against you are the restrictions in the **lease** or renting agreement. Leases can be fearsome legal documents, and it is wise to seek a solicitor's advice on its contents. The set working for you are the **Landlord and Tenant Acts**. Just as private tenants are protected by law from the excesses of their landlords, so are business tenants. Legal requirements must be met before tenants can be given notice to quit, and sometimes landlords have to pay compensation. Proper procedures must be followed when the rent is increased. It's worth getting legal advice then too.

13 *Tax, VAT, an* *insurance*

U NLESS YOU WANT to be a 'ghost' you must allow for tax when working out your gains from the business. This applies not only for VAT and the tax on profits, but also for long-term savings and arrangements such as a pension or life assurance. A 'ghost', in tax jargon, is someone who for official purposes does not exist and never pays taxes. Unless your profits are too low, you will be paying tax. You should also be planning to ensure you can afford to retire in due course, and provide your family with some security if anything happens to you. As the tax system helps pay for private pensions and some savings, while also collecting contributions for state pensions, the two topics can be looked at together.

These are topics of considerable detail but continuing importance. Because of that, I have written a companion book to this one, *Don't Pay Too Much Tax If You're Self-Employed*. It covers VAT and all the taxes fully, with some account of social security law as well. Consequently, the coverage in this section is in outline only.

When you decide to launch your business, notify:

The **VAT Office** of Customs and Excise if you need to register for VAT (which you must do if your sales are high enough);

The **Inland Revenue**, who collect income and corporation taxes from your business and any person you employ (and usually NI contributions as well);

The **DSS** and its executive agency the **Contributions Agency** through your local **Social Security Office,** to deal with your NI contributions and benefit entitlement, and those of any person you employ.

How do you do this, and when?

If your total turnover of goods and services liable to VAT will be greater than £45,000 in the next month (note that this figure is correct for 1994, but changes each year) or was over £45,000 in the last year, you must register for VAT with the local VAT Office (address in the phone book). Total turnover means the total sale price of all goods and the total charge price for all services, if those goods or services are liable to VAT.

REGISTERING FOR VAT

What goods and services are liable to VAT? Almost all goods are subject to VAT (including zero-rate VAT on food, books, children's clothes and exports). The main exceptions are linked to health and welfare services. Most forms of services are also subject to VAT, but financial and insurance services are exempt, as are most rents, and most health, education and welfare services. Services for overseas customers tend to be taxed overseas. There is a full list in **Customs Notice VAT 700, The VAT Guide.** Get a free copy. The VAT Offices publish a full series of leaflets about VAT. You should also get **Should I Be Registered For VAT?** And, if you are a retailer, **Customs Notice 727, Retail Schemes**. You register by filling in form **VAT 1** available from all VAT Offices.

You **must** register for VAT within 30 days of realising that your turnover will exceed the limits in the next month, or that it has done so in the last year. You have to pay VAT anyway, even if you don't register. You would also be liable for penalties for not registering. Either get your accountants on to this, or get in touch with the VAT Office in good time if it applies to you.

You are entitled to register for VAT even if you are not required to do so, provided that you are in business and that you are making or intend to make supplies of goods or services that are liable to VAT. Registering is sometimes an advantage, for example if you anticipate having to register in due course, or if it is better from the point of view of your customers that you are registered. Again, an accountant or the VAT Office can give you advice on this.

TELLING THE REVENUE

You must advise the Revenue that you have started business on your own account (or about your company, if there is a new one) by the end of the first year of business. The best way of doing this is to ask the office of the local H M Inspector of Taxes (see under Inland Revenue in the phone book) for leaflet **IR28, Starting in Business**. This has a form at the back, **41G**, to be sent in to the local tax office. It covers all the tax issues that need sorting out. The Revenue publish many other useful leaflets as well. Get : **IR53, Thinking of Taking Someone On? PAYE** for Employers and **IR57, Thinking of Working for Yourself?**, also **CGT11, Capital Gains Tax and the Small Businessman**, to learn something of another tax you need to watch.

Three things covered by form 41G need checking from the start. First, are you appointing accountants (if your business is a company, you will be doing so anyway)? If so, it may be best for them also to handle your **tax compliance** work (as accountants call sorting accounts out with the Revenue). Good accountants will more than pay back their fees doing this!

Second, choose the date to which you make up your first set of accounts carefully. You can save money by doing so if you are a sole trader or a partnership. This is because you pay tax on the profits for a year covered by your accounts in the year containing the day the accounts close. Whether your accounts end on 30 April 1994 or 31 March 1995, you will pay the tax due on the same dates (as the tax year starts on 6 April each year). An end-April accounts year means you keep the tax for almost a year longer. Again, if you have accountants, check with them.

Finally, if you are employing anyone whom you are paying more than about £55 a week (the figure is reviewed from year to year), you must tell the Revenue. You are required to collect income tax from employees under the **PAYE** (Pay As You Earn) system. So accept my congratulations now. If you go into business, you will swiftly be appointed as one of H M Collectors of Taxes (honorary of course). And don't think you can get out of it by not telling them. If you should have collected the tax, and did not do so, **you** owe the tax, not the employee.

If you intend to be a labour only sub-contractor in the **construction industry**, you need a tax certificate before you can get paid by your main contractors without losing tax on the payment. Get leaflet **IR14, Tax Deductions Scheme Explanatory Booklet** to find out more.

LETTING THE DSS KNOW

If you are going to be self-employed, inform your local Social Security Office (address in phone book). Also tell them if you are going to employ anyone earning over about £60 in any week from you. You have to collect NI contributions from those employees under the PAYE scheme, and also pay contributions yourself on their earnings. You also need to sort out your own contribution liability.

To find out about this, and get the relevant forms, get the following leaflets from your local Social Security Office: **NI22, Stamping and Returning Contribution Cards for those Paying Class 2 and Class 3 contributions; NI27A, People with Small Earnings from Self-Employment; NI41, NI guidance for the Self-Employed; NI 255, Class 2 and Class 3 Contributions - the Easy Way to Pay!; NP15, Employers' Guide to NI Contributions; NP18, Class 4 contributions**. By way of translation, Class 1 contributions are those paid by employees and their employers (and Class 1A are also paid by employers), Class 2 is the flat-rate self-employed contribution, Class 4 is the earnings-related self-employed contribution (in effect extra income tax), and Class 3 is the voluntary contribution for those not in employment.

If you have employees paying NI contributions, you are also responsible for paying any **statutory**

sick pay or **statutory maternity pay** due to them. Get : **NI227, Employers' guide to statutory sick pay** and **NI257, Employers' guide to statutory maternity pay**, to find out more.

If you are registered for VAT, you will need to keep detailed records and make regular returns to the VAT Office. You will also need to do this if employing anyone for whom PAYE or NI contributions have to be paid. You will also need records for tax as your profits grow.

However, the tax office only requires the simplest of accounts from the smallest businesses. If your total turnover is below £15,000, you are required only to state the turnover, the total of expenses, and the taxable profit (the difference). Should this be queried, you could be asked for full records to prove the basis of these figures, but that is not normal practice.

It is worth paying attention to tax rules, because you can easily pay more tax than needed. Sometimes, people pay more than even the government intends. We cover this in detail in *Don't Pay Too Much Tax If You're Self-Employed*. One or two ideas will indicate the sorts of point that arise.

If Husband is self-employed and Wife is not at work, H should pay W for helping in the business a weekly amount that is below the lower figure on which employees pay NI contributions (£57 is the limit in 1994). If she earns less than that, W has to pay no NI contributions or (if she has no other earned income) income tax. H also has to pay no NI contributions as her employer. However, the cost of paying W is deductible from H's business expenses. If H wants to pay W more than these amounts, he can do it as non-taxable benefits in kind, or as pension contributions. W must, of course, have a job to do for H.

H also employs part-time staff. One, E, earns about £60 a week. If E earns £60 a week, E and H both have to pay NI contributions. H pays at 3.6 per cent, and E pays at 2 per cent on the first £57, and 10 per cent above that. At these rates, E pays £1.44, so gets £58.56, while H pays £62.16 including the NI contributions. E also pays tax at 20 per cent on the first £60 over, say, £65 a week, so will pay no income tax unless the earnings are increased. If H gave E free meals and other benefits in kind, so that the earnings were below £57 in cash, then all NI contributions would be avoided. Similarly, if H wants to give E a pay rise then no income tax must be paid if the extra benefits are in non-taxable form, for example free meals or the loan of clothes.

PLANNING FINANCES AHEAD

I expect, like me, you plan to retire sometime. How are you going to be able to afford it? State pensions are only a safety-net and in any event will be worth nothing like as much then as now. Why? At and beyond the end of the century there will be more retired people, and fewer people at work paying NI contributions. So we cannot then afford the level of pensions we pay out now. The moral is simple: if you want a better standard of living than that, you must buy it in the meantime.

Think also what would happen if you were

killed in an accident, or maimed so you could not carry on your business? Who would look after your wife/widow (it may be even worse for widowers) and any small children? Pensions for widows will be cut along with the retirement pension, and for the same unavoidable reason. Even now, are widow's pensions as good as your family's standard of living?

A PERSONAL PENSION

When starting a small business, and strapped for cash, financing pensions and insurance against personal disaster looks like a luxury. In reality, it is a trade-off - earnings now or earnings then. What makes it a direct trade-off are the tax rules. If you pay money into an approved pension or assurance scheme, and you are either self-employed or your money is going into a personal pension, you get a tax deduction for the money going into the fund. The fund pays no income tax or capital gains tax on its profits while the money is in the fund. You only pay when the money comes back out again as income - lump sums can be free of tax even then.

Even a cautious start on a pensions policy will be something for which you are most grateful 20 years on. Get quotes on a self-employed pension scheme from insurance companies and brokers, and find out how much it will cost you. Payments are usually monthly, and can vary from year to year with the profits.

LIFE AND HEALTH
INSURANCE

Think also what will happen to your business if you die or are unable to work any more. And if you are in business with partners or fellow directors of a company, what would happen if any of them suddenly died. Don't think it doesn't happen. Three years ago, I took over heading my department one Sunday because my predecessor had died without warning the previous afternoon. Each partner's life and director's life should be insured against the loss to the business from their death. It's called **key man insurance**. You should have **life assurance** to protect your family from the financial calamity that might hit them if you were killed - for example, in a situation where you have borrowed to invest in a business, and those borrowings are not fully covered by the business assets. If these debts became due on your death , your family could pay them off with the proceeds from a life assurance policy.

Besides life insurance, find out about **insurance against disability or ill-health**. Remember, once you are self-employed there is no big employer standing behind you to pay you while you get better. You can claim **state sickness benefit**, and should do so straight away if you are ill and off work, but that is only a small help. **Medical expenses insurance** will allow you more flexibility in getting treatment at times that affect your work less.

You can insure against almost any risk. As every major disaster shows, many people assume it will never happen to them. It does. The trouble is, once it <u>has</u> happened, the financial problems of being uninsured may prevent them ever getting finances sorted out afterwards. What is more, you get full **tax relief** for all insurance premiums to protect the business - but you don't get full tax relief if you have to spend out money to replace something damaged in a disaster.

BUSINESS INSURANCE

Before it happens to you, here is a checklist of kinds of insurance you should consider having. First, three forms of **compulsory insurance** - cover you must have:

Employer's liability insurance – you must be insured against liability to any employee who is injured because of your carelessness, or that of any other employee. And you must display the insurance certificate at the workplace.

Road traffic insurance – your business vehicles must be insured for passenger and other third party cover.

Premises insurance – not required by law, but it is normally required either from a business tenant by a landlord, or by anyone lending money on the premises under a mortgage, to cover rebuilding costs from a fire or other disaster.

Other aspects of your business you should also consider insuring include:

Fire - to cover the contents too

Special Perils - to cover things normally left out of fire policies, such as bursting water tanks

All risks - to make your policy even wider than that, covering accidents, for example

Theft from buildings or vehicles (other than shoplifting or by staff)

Money in buildings, on staff or otherwise

Goods in transit - what happens if the

delivery lorry crashes, or the post gets lost?

Business interruption - not only is your building damaged by a fire, but you may also have to shut down for a period. Who pays the wages then?

Liability - We've already covered employer's liability. There is also **public liability** (eg when a customer slips on your newly-washed shop floor and breaks a leg) and **product liability** (eg when due to a mistake in manufacture the clothes you sell irritate people's skins badly)

Engineering - to cover breakdown of machinery, including computers

Credit insurance against bad debts

Fidelity - is aimed to protect you from dishonest employees

Legal expenses - helps meet the legal costs bill if you get involved in legal actions

Travel - when you are injured by accidents while travelling.

This checklist is taken from the **Small Business Advice Files** produced by the Association of British Insurers. Get a copy from them or from insurance companies or brokers. Once you have decided at what level you should be insuring each kind of risk, get quotes from several companies. Many companies sell packaged policies covering the needs of the average small business. These may suit you well, but check whether you have special needs not covered by the usual policy.

Once you have obtained insurance cover, you need to keep an eye on two aspects of the insurance. First, make sure you review the level of cover from time to time, both as values change and as your business grows, to ensure you remain fully insured. If you insure only half the value of the business, don't be surprised if the insurance company pay out only half your claim. The other point is to note the terms of the insurance policy, and any requirements imposed on you. Do you need to take certain safety measures to make a claim valid? Do thefts have to be reported promptly to the police? Is there a time limit within which claims must be made?

KEEP YOUR POLICIES
UNDER REVIEW

14   *Employees*

F IRING STAFF is never fun. It can also be expensive on your funds, time and standing with other employees. Not firing someone who ought to go is even more expensive. That is one reason you should take great care to employ the right people for the right jobs. A better reason is that your staff are your best assets, and deserve and need the best management.

LET THE PERSON FIT THE JOB

When you need employees (other than members of your family) sort out three things before you appoint anyone:

A **job description** for each job;

The **terms and conditions** on which each job is offered;

The **qualifications** needed by anyone holding the job

Establish these first, and you are more likely to appoint, and keep, the right person.

The clearer and better these are, the less room there is for staff to dispute what they are supposed to be doing. Work out your own standard document for all staff. Think about the following:

Title of job

Purpose of job

Duties to be performed

Special tasks assigned to job-holder

Responsibilities of job-holder

To whom job-holder answers

Who answers to job-holder

Authority of job-holder

Everyone should be given a job description at the start, and the contents should be made clear during the appointing process. That gives you both a point of reference. The description also lets you think about what hours the job requires. Do you want full-time staff? Part-time staffing may give you more flexibility.

Decide what bargain you are striking for the job, and make this clear to any appointee during the appointment - not afterwards. Better still, write it down. The law requires you to give an employee a statement of the terms of employment within 13 weeks of starting with you, unless you have already set all the terms out in writing. The statement must include the following: job title; date job started; date employee first worked for you; pay, and basis of calculation; hours of work; holidays and entitlement to holiday pay; arrangements during sickness, including sick pay; any pension; period of notice, or length of employment if it is fixed term; procedure to deal with grievances.

Generally, terms and conditions are for agreement between you and each employee. In practice there are many limits to this. If there is an agreement between employers' federations and unions, you will probably want to go along with that.

LEGAL REQUIREMENTS

All employees are entitled to minimum periods of notice and to be treated without racial or sexual discrimination, including equal pay for men and women doing work of equal value. Staff paying NI contributions are entitled to statutory sick pay and, in appropriate cases, statutory maternity pay, and may be entitled to maternity leave. Entitlement to some of these requirements only arises after employees have worked for 2 years, and maternity leave can only be claimed if proper notice is given.

Under the 1986 Wages Act you must give staff a statement of how their pay is made up when paying them, including details of tax and other deductions. Fines or pay reductions, as far as permitted under that Act, must be agreed with the staff concerned. Staff are entitled to have safe working conditions. You can be liable in the criminal courts for failing to provide this. You should also ensure your premises comply with the standards of the Fire Precautions Act (check this with your local Fire Service). If you have more than 4 employees, you must adopt a written health and safety policy. The **Department of Employment**, the **Equal Opportunities Commission**, the **Commission for Racial Equality**, and the **Health and Safety Commission** all provide free leaflets setting out

the requirements in detail. They will offer
further guidance.

Decide what are the minimum requirements for
each job. Then you can set about finding the
staff, making clear what is expected of them.
You could use recruitment agencies, but they
can be quite expensive. So can the long-term use
of staff obtained through the 'temp' agencies -
though for very short jobs that may be a good
answer. Find out their rates before using them.
For some jobs it may be better to use **sub-
contractors** rather than hire your own staff. This
may also save you having to buy expensive
equipment   or   tools   if   the   sub-
contractor will supply these.

Hiring staff is often still a remarkably hit-and-
miss affair. For straightforward jobs this may not
matter, if you are satisfied about the employee's
basic abilities. Appointment of your senior
manager on the basis of a short interview and
shorter letter of application is decidedly risky.
Take careful steps to get a broader picture by
arranging more than one interview, getting
references, making informal enquiries, and
encouraging prospective employees to do the
same. Use your interviews well, making sure you
cover all the important points, and giving the
candidate plenty of chance to talk. And treat the
candidates well. Why create unnecessary
enemies?

Too many employers assume, once a member of
staff is appointed, that that is that. Review the
post regularly so the employee can, and wants
to, give of his or her best to the business. Most
people want both to work well and to know that
they are doing so. They will get satisfaction out

HIRING THE STAFF

HELPING STAFF

of doing a good job. It gives most people their identity. Think why you wanted to go into your business - was it dissatisfaction with your employer? Make sure, above all, you are a good boss, and your staff will repay your efforts.

Being a good boss depends partly on making clear to staff what is expected of them, and then - in a very positive way - appraising them fairly to see if they are doing this. They should be told on regular reviews - perhaps every year - how they are doing. If they are doing really well, they should be told so. If not, they should be told clearly what is going wrong, and helped to put it right. Targets can be set and attainment rewarded. And don't skimp on the training. Above all, treat them with confidence so that they see what they are supposed to be doing. Managing staff well does not just happen - it needs planning, too, and an acceptance that the 'other side' is not another side at all. Your staff have the same broad feelings and attitudes as you.

FIRING STAFF

Hopefully, if you planned your job descriptions right, and chose wisely, and then helped positively, not much of this needs to be done. If it does, follow a fair and thorough procedure, and the law will support you rather than hinder you. If not, you can be taken to the Industrial Tribunal for unfair dismissal. An employee cannot take you to an Industrial Tribunal until he or she has worked for you for two years. That gives you a period during which the employee's suitability can be assessed.

If staff are unsatisfactory, make sure they know why. Tell them why, pointing out the rules. It is good practice to give written warnings of this, and ask staff to sign copies to show they have received the warnings. But give them a chance to explain and see whether things can be improved. Then give them a chance to sort things out. If you are still dissatisfied, give a second written warning, pointing out clearly the consequences if there is no improvement, and making sure they know what is required of them. If after all this they still do not meet the requirements, give them proper notice under their contracts. Best practice will be to confirm this in writing, giving reasons for dismissal. If you follow a systematic and fair approach, there is little danger of your being found to have dismissed someone unfairly.

If someone has been in gross breach of his terms of employment - stealing from the business, physical violence on others at work or similar reasons - **instant dismissal** is probably acceptable. But make sure you have explored the circumstances, if you were not there at the time.

AFTER EMPLOYEES
LEAVE

When staff leave, tell the tax authorities. If your employee claims social security, you will probably be asked why the job ended. If you say the job ended because the employee left voluntarily without good reason, or he or she was fired because of misconduct, the employee may lose unemployment benefit for up to 26 weeks. There may also be no income support during that period. This can be a severe penalty.

If you are asked to give a **reference** for an ex-employee make sure it is honest. If it is too good and misleads a future employer, he could sue you for negligent misstatement. If it is deliberately and maliciously bad, the employee could sue you for defamation. If you do not wish to give a bad reference, it is better to stay silent.

15 *Outside help*

M OST PEOPLE running small businesses are do-it-yourself experts. I do not mean that they are very good at mending the secretaries' kettle, or repairing the delivery van. No doubt they can do all these, but they probably have better things to do with their time. Rather, they have to be their own buyers, sales team, public relations advisers, production engineers, personnel officers, safety officers...the list seems endless. Not for them is the luxury of the large corporation, which can hire an expert team to handle every facet of the business.

The danger, as with all DIY, is that self-sufficiency gets carried too far. In writing this book I have relied on the advice of others running small businesses and experts in several fields. You should be doing the same in getting your business going. Even if you want to go it entirely alone, in practice you can't get far without some outside help. For example, help from an accountant, a solicitor, a bank or an insurance expert may prove unavoidable. So act positive, and get them on your side from the start.

Do not assume it will cost you a fortune. Advice from several of the sources below is free. Some may even give _you_ money. Those that do charge will often save you more money than they cost you, provided you know what you want from them. Nonetheless the charge rates of expert professionals are often £100 an hour or more. Wasting their time is wasting your money. Nor should you assume their time is free, unless they say so. Not every bank manager charges a customer for the time taken enjoying the customer's invitation to lunch, but it has been done! It pays to get estimates of costs from any professional.

Who can help, and how? We first look at the advisers that you should consider appointing to work with you, and then the sources of help and advice available through government and other agencies.

The wealth of help and assistance that can be gained by anyone setting up in business is considerable, but your need for expert assistance does not stop there. You will, in addition, and from the beginning, need the services of your own professionals. In particular you will probably need accounting help, a bank, legal advice, and insurance advice.

APPOINTING YOUR OWN EXPERTS

All these services now compete strongly for the favour of the small business owner. Most offer a far wider range of services than they traditionally used to, with growing competition. Their aim increasingly is the 'one-stop shop' where all advice is available. But there are still things each can do that the other professions cannot usually do as well, and you may need to form your own team. If so, do that at the beginning. Do not leave appointing your lawyer or accountant until you know you have hit a problem. They will probably discover that you have also hit several others you did not know about.

ACCOUNTANTS

It is said, only half in fun, that when choosing an accountant, go into the office with your books and ask the accountant to find what your profits are. Don't appoint the person who promptly sits down with a calculator and works it out for you - appoint instead the one who says 'What figure do you want?' More seriously, you may need someone to help you run the finances of the business, to sort out tax and VAT questions, to make sure your books are keeping a true record of your business, to check the validity of your accounts each year, and perhaps to check on the financial viability of your plans.

Strictly, you are only required by law to appoint an accountant if your business is run through a company. If so, you need an auditor for your company accounts, and this is a major job of accountants. As already noted, this requirement is going to be removed for the smallest companies. However, unless you know what you are doing, you should still consider appointing one for these companies or if you are a sole trader. You will probably need one for a partnership.

Anyone can call herself or himself an accountant. The only qualification for having the word in a letterhead is having the money to pay for printing it! Protect yourself by appointing someone who is a member of the major accounting institutions. They impose high standards on all entrants, impose codes of conduct and have professional insurance schemes to protect you against losing money through an accountant's professional errors. Talk to a number of accountants about what you want and what they have to offer.

Accounting firms vary enormously in size and coverage. The largest are huge businesses with branches in every major city in the world. They specialise not only in accounting and auditing but equally in taxation, management consultancy, personnel selection, technical training, aspects of legal compliance, business formation, development financing, import and export work, payroll and pension problems, and so on... far removed from the one-person band, able to offer a much more limited service, but doing it personally and locally.

Check that the accountant belongs to an appropriate professional association. The main ones are: **CA** or **FCA** - the Institutes of Chartered Accountants (there are separate English, Scottish and Irish institutes). Chartered accountants must undergo rigorous training plus a three-year training period before qualifying. Most are graduates. The other major body is the Chartered Association of Certified Accountants (**FCCA** or **ACCA**). **CIMA**, the Institute of Management Accountants is a more specialist body whose members may be of assistance.

How do you choose? The best way to start is by seeking personal recommendations. Ask others with similar problems whom they would get to do the work, and why. Another point to watch: your interests may be best served by a smaller firm. There you should be not just another client, but make sure there is someone qualified to look after you if your usual accountant is ill or on holiday. You may find best service from a larger firm that has specialist skills and contacts in your area of business, for example a local office in a country to which you intend to export.

If you are thinking of buying someone else's business, accountants are trained in the mumbo-jumbo and hidden problems in a set of business accounts. You should get them to read the accounts. This is management accounting; that is, the use of the figures to analyse the strengths and weaknesses of a business to plan ahead, so that the business can be developed in ways that exploit those strengths and eliminate the weaknesses. Ordinary accounts tell you whether you made a profit or a loss. Management accounts should show which parts of your business made the most profits, and how much, the effects of changes in your business, and where your overheads seem too high.

Finally, fees. There is no fixed basis for accountancy fees, though firms usually base them on time spent and the hourly charge rate of the person devoting time to your work. Each visit, letter and telephone call is charged at the rate appropriate to a partner or trainee, as the case may be. But you can still ask for estimates or even tenders, as competition is strong.

LEGAL ADVICE

Your legal advisers are best chosen before you suddenly need them for some legal action. As with accountants, there are a few jobs for which in practical terms employing a lawyer is unavoidable, but there are many other services that a commercially-minded solicitor can offer. Look at the amount of law in other parts of this book: hiring and sacking staff; getting permission for your business; getting your contract terms right; making sure your business structure is right... as well as court cases and property transfers.

Unlike accountancy, lawyers run a closed profession. People cannot call themselves **'solicitor'** unless they have passed the Law Society's examinations and served a training contract. Further, before they set up on their own, they must serve three further years working as an assistant to another solicitor. All solicitors acting for the public must have a practising certificate that must be renewed yearly. They must also comply with strict financial regulations and a code of ethics, and must be insured against causing their clients losses. **Barristers**, who handle court work and give specialist advice on the law, can only be instructed by a solicitor or other professional, so cannot be approached directly by a businessman. There are others who have set up paralegal services or legal advice clinics without being qualified. Frankly, they are best avoided.

Law firms tend to specialise or, in the bigger firms, have specialist departments. Solicitors now advertise, and should tell you what services they cover. Many bigger firms have brochures describing who they are and what they do. Some will not deal with business matters at all, concentrating perhaps on divorce or criminal work. Make sure your solicitors are used to dealing with small businesses. The points about size and cost made about accountants apply equally here.

Appoint your lawyers early. For example, if buying into a franchise, get their advice on the franchise contract. If setting up a partnership, get advice about it at the beginning. If getting new premises, you will need a solicitor to do the conveyancing. You should certainly get one to read and advise on the terms of any lease you are asked to sign. It is standard lawyer's advice never to sign anything you have not read. But have you ever tried reading a ninety-page lease? Don't. Get them to look at it for you. Further, a good lawyer's many contacts, as those of a good accountant, may prove useful to your business in wider ways.

BANKS

Banks have been developing very rapidly in recent years in help for small businesses. Indeed, it has been almost too easy for some to get money out of them. On the other hand, someone once defined a banker as a person who would lend you his umbrella when the sun was shining, but demand it back the moment it starts raining. He's still right. Perhaps the difference now is that they are more prepared to endure the summer showers before recalling the umbrella. But not always.

The big banks have completely revised their approach to smaller customers in recent years. They now offer you attractive literature and helpful advice. Further, they have often transferred their business customers to business units so that they can concentrate on giving advice. Equally, they are keen to sell you their wider services, and their fees for help need to be watched as closely as those of accountants and lawyers.

Even if you do not want the bank's wider services, you will still need a good banker - unless you believe that money, not springs, makes the best stuffing for a mattress. However small and simple your business, you need reliable bank accounts. You will need cheques and credit transfers cleared and honoured with speed and without query. This is always better done through separate business accounts and not your personal accounts. That way you can keep a check on the business funds. If you are handling large amounts of your customers' money, separate accounts may be wise. These can be linked with deposit accounts so the money does not lie idle.

Like it or not, your bank manager will soon learn a lot about you and your finances. It helps to let them know what you are doing, and get the advice they can offer. You will find that a manager is often willing to talk generally when you first meet, and probably has some useful tips about local business. But remember also that, unlike the accountant or lawyer who is employed by you and for you, the bank remains an independent concern that is selling you its products. It is not paid to be *your* adviser and has always to look after its own interests first.

You will, fairly early on, have to buy at least some insurance. Even then you should be planning for the future and in case things go wrong. You therefore probably need to get advice on insurance. Under the Financial Services Act all those advising on finance and insurance need to be authorised to do so, and must either sell only their own products or only other people's. You may be able to get advice from your bank, accountant or lawyer, but it may pay to shop around more. You also need to think about liability insurance to cover business risks and general insurance of your property, equipment and staff.

INSURANCE ADVISERS

You can either get your insurance direct from the insurance **companies,** or through insurance **brokers**, who are agents selling insurance for several companies. They will normally offer you advice on what they think you need, and then find you what they think to be the best value policy for you. Insurance brokers get commission from the insurance companies for selling their policies. They can shop around for you and give you a choice of insurance cover. Other insurance companies prefer to sell direct to the customer, cutting out the middleman's commission. As with anything else, it pays to look for the best bargains. One thing that is **not** a bargain is not bothering to insure.

Accountants, lawyers, bankers and insurance advisers should constitute your back-up team of professional advisers. In addition, you will probably need other professionals to help from time to time. You can also get more general help from a variety of public sources.

HELP FROM GOVERNMENT

Government aid for new businesses has itself been repackaged in recent years. The main focus of provision in England and Wales is now the TECs or **Training and Enterprise Councils**. (They are called Local Enterprise Companies (LECs) in Scotland.) These are organised through the DTI - Department of Trade and Industry. They offer local courses and counselling and advice (contact details at end of book).

TECs operate at regional level, and as general agencies. Most immediate provision in nearly every part of the country comes from the nearest of several hundred **Local Enterprise Agencies.** These invaluable (to the community) and free (to the small businessman) bodies have sprung up all over Britain in the last few years. Their strength is that they are local bodies set up to meet local needs. As a result, they have no one way of working. Nor do they have any set form of name, though they are usually named after their localities. They do have the same objective - to offer advice and help to those wanting to set up on their own in that area. Funding comes from the TECs and donations from councils, local businesses and charities. They also have staff seconded to them by major businesses so can provide their services free to the new business. Their focus lies in giving advice by business people to business people. For example, they will help work through your business plan with you.

If you cannot easily find the name of your local enterprise agency, contact **Business in the Community** (address at end), the national body coordinating LEAs (for short).

An LEA can offer initial help on any aspect of your business that you can think of, and then those you haven't thought about. It is staffed by people with direct experience, and has a wide circle of contacts on which it can draw, ranging from grant-making bodies to local councils. Because it is a mixture of both public sector and private sector, it also has contacts with the local professions, banks and others whose help you need. Its staff will counsel you on what you ought, and ought not, be doing, and, if felt necessary, warn you off what they feel to be bad ideas. For the great majority the enterprise agency will offer encouragement and support. Either way, seek their help at an early stage.

TECs and LEAs also often run courses on aspects of running your own business, both for those just thinking of starting and for those who have got going. They continue to help as the business develops - though, as one manager put it, they don't so often get people coming back. Those who are succeeding may assume they don't need any further help. Those who are failing may assume they will just be made to feel foolish. Neither is true. Both still need help, and will get it.

Besides these agencies, training is now offered by a range of commercial and voluntary concerns. Local universities and colleges often run short courses as well. The TECs can assist in finding out about these, through a computer database and your local **Training Access Point.**

Other help is also available through the **DTI**, which is responsible for both regional grants and for international and export assistance and with trade links with the European Union. They may be contacted by telephoning ENTERPRISE INITIATIVE on 0800 500 200.

Government help for rural areas is channelled through the **Rural Development Commission** in England. Help in the other countries is also available through **ATB Scotland**, the **Welsh Development Agency** and the Northern Ireland **Local Enterprise Development Unit.**

LOCAL COUNCILS

Some local councils provide a great deal of help - including financial help - to small businesses in their areas. These councils have special units (often called **Economic Development Units**) for the job. They can help not just with dealing with other departments of the council (such as the planners) but other local contacts as well. Other councils content themselves with advertising the joys of working in their area with no direct back-up (though they may give financial support to the local enterprise agency to do that instead). Others just rest on their laurels, and are content for you to rest on yours. That's one reason why the section on location in this book is important.

One much neglected free local service you should make a point of using is your **local library** service. If you are one of those who assumes that a library is merely a place to borrow tatty novels you are missing valuable help. Libraries might be better called **information centres** (as a few are) because they provide access to a tremendous amount of useful information, as we see in 'What are you selling?'

If your local library is small, it is part of a chain linked to the county (or city) commercial or **business library**. The London Business Library or Manchester Commercial Library, for example, are superb collections of reference books and journals spanning the world. Library staff will suggest where you can find the details about your own query. More generally, you will find books such as this one and more specialist volumes on the open shelves - usually under **classification number 658.** (If that's where you got this from in the first place, find out about the rest of the library's facilities when you take it back).

For the young:

Government help, such as the new enterprise allowance scheme, is aimed primarily at those aged at least 18. The assumption is that YTS (the Youth Training Scheme) is the best avenue for those who leave full-time education before that. **Careers Office** help will be available for those wanting to aim at their own business from the start.

The **Prince's Youth Business Trust** provides advice, training and financial assistance for those aged 18 to 25 setting up or developing their own business. It works both direct and through local agencies and youth organisations. Help starts with advice on a business plan, but can include grants of up to £1,000 a person, or £3,000 a business, with loans also available.

One private scheme that is open for those aged from 16 is **Livewire**. This is a competition in form, for developing the best business ideas. Although only some get the prizes, everyone can gain because counselling and advice is available to all participants throughout the period of the competition. Two other initiatives offering advice and support are **Headstart** and **Instant Muscle**. Headstart is aimed at those aged 17 to 25, and its main support is through part-time training and helping with your business plan, and help from a counsellor for a year. Instant Muscle is aimed at getting help to the young in deprived city areas. In Wales, the **Youth Initiative Programme**, run by the Welsh Development Agency, aims straight at those in and leaving school. Its sessions start in schools and can be followed by further sessions with business counsellors for those interested in going into their own businesses. (For addresses see end.)

For minority communities:

Whilst none of the agencies so far described discriminates in any way, sadly the community often does. To help those minorities caught by this, **Project Fullemploy** has as one of its aims helping those aged 18-30 from minority ethnic origins to get started in self-employment (address at end). Some local authorities will also give special help to the minority groups.

For the disabled:

Special help and advice is available through Jobcentres from the government's **Disablement Advisory Service** and **Disablement Resettlement Officers** for those who find their work impaired, or difficult because of a disability. Help is also available through the agencies noted above. A private organisation that can also offer help is the **Disabled Living Foundation** (address at end).

In particular industries:

Contact the Industry Training Board, if there is one. Help may also be forthcoming through the **trade association** relevant to your business - get the address through your local library. One industry given particular support is tourism (also one of the UK's fastest growing industries). Financial support, advice and support are available through the national **Tourist Boards** (addresses at end). Your local enterprise agency or TEC will also be able to tell you about other help specific to your kind of business, including special courses and grant schemes.

16   *Expanding*

B USINESSES HAVE LIFE-SPANS like everything else. However, the speed at which they grow up - and grow old - depends far less on nature than on those running them. Whatever uncertainties await, one thing is guaranteed. Once started, your business will never stand still. It will always be changing. Your job is to plan and manage that change, so that the business goes on growing and renewing itself. To grow big is not of itself the aim. What is needed is a good cashflow and growing profits. That can come in two ways: increasing the **efficiency** of the business, and increasing its **scale**.

MAKE THE BUSINESS MORE EFFICIENT

At first, the main job of a business is to get going. It needs to acquire customers as fast as it can properly cope with them to produce a positive cashflow and then an operating profit. Hopefully, it will grow fast. Whatever the speed, some activities will be more profitable than others. Once the business is going, growth and profitability must be kept under review. Monitor profitability so that attention can be concentrated on the high-margin products. Also monitor general business administration so that excess general overheads can be trimmed.

The accounts and product costing should show where the high margin business is and if any products sell at a loss. The customer base, or 'bank' as it is sometimes called, also needs monitoring. Is there a particularly good group of customers emerging? If so, should your efforts be concentrated more on them? Should you be expanding the product range of those things which that sort of customer wants, whilst holding other sales more steady? Or are you, after an initial spurt, relying only on established customers, without sufficient new ones being introduced?

The point here is that market research is a continuing operation, not just a one-off. Whatever you do, the market will not stand still. Similarly, your advertising and selling effort needs assessing to see if it is supporting the most effective parts of the business, or if parts need boosting.

The other area to monitor is general overheads. It is a fundamental law of physics that order always degenerates into chaos. It applies to businesses as much as to atoms. Hence one of those laws attributed to Murphy: left to themselves, business costs always rise until they are overhead. The answer is to constantly reimpose order. One way the business can do this is to borrow the skills of the physicist, and get a computer in.

LET TECHNOLOGY
CHIP IN

Computers and similar advances cannot be

ignored. The first edition of this book was written on a computer, but a tiny one. The second edition was written on a much better one that is now completely obsolescent, and has been replaced by the yet more powerful one I am now using, a 486 with fast processing speed and a huge memory. What can it do with all those features? Any of the following :

Word processor (with a built-in spelling check, grammar check, and dictionary, and quite good enough to produce a news-sheet or posters).

Spreadsheet - an electronic worksheet which does the sums as you go along. Combined, the two are used to produce ready-made sets of **business accounts**.

Database - a highly efficient way of holding information, ideal for holding mailing lists that can be used selectively. Information about or for customers can be stored for quick access. Computer-based stock-holding lists are also increasingly familiar. It can also be merged with information in the word processor to produce personalised letters to a range of people.

Graphics - anything from the mock-up account book pages in this text to complicated CAD (computer-aided design for engineers and architects) applications. You can also get software to help with sales and technical presentations.

An organiser - a computer-based version of a filofax and diary, with organisation charts.

Don't get carried away with the computer as a

new toy. Before you get one, check what precisely needs doing. The first stage of introducing a computer is **systems analysis** - and that can be done with advantage anywhere, even if you don't want a computer. This means analysing the system of work into each of its stages, to see what can be automated, and how. In theory, you then get the computer to do all those jobs which can be left to it.

In practice, things don't work like that. Specially written computer programs can be enormously expensive, and full of teething problems and bugs. Being realistic, you need to find the **software** (as the programs are universally called) to suit your business. There are an increasing number of sophisticated small business packages available combining, within limits, all the functions set out above. One problem is those limits. Nothing is worse than spending ages getting all your accounts transferred on to a computer, only to find a year later it is not big enough and you have to start again. In practice, the limits on modern software are now getting beyond the range of normal human demands. Yet the prices of the main products of firms like Microsoft are falling sharply.

Only when you know you can get a software package that suits your needs should you then set about getting the **hardware** you need. This will include the computer itself, backed by a good memory capacity (hard disks are now so cheap that there is no point in avoiding a large one), a monitor (get one that is good for your eyes), and a printer that handles graphics. There are plenty of magazines that give you a good idea of current prices, which can be anything from a few hundred pounds (less tax relief) upwards. One other thing to look for is a system that will need the minimum time down - out of action - and that can be backed up, that is, you

BEGIN AT THE END

have a stand-by in case something goes wrong with it. You only find out by experience just how frustrating it is to wipe out a whole year's budget through some minor fault, only to discover you have no other copy. I have, and recommend you don't.

Properly used, a computer can speed up your accounting and clerical jobs, make your marketing information more usable, keep tabs on your stock and outstanding bills, improve the quality of your letters and publications and allow you to keep a tighter check on what is going on.

GET REGISTERED

If you use a computer to keep any information about anyone else (customers, mailing lists, employee files or other personal information), you must register under the Data Protection Act. Get in touch with the **Data Protection Registry** (address at end). They will send you the relevant forms and explanatory books. The Registry keeps a public register of all those with computer-based databanks of personal information. You may demand to see register entries, and can demand from anyone who is registered copies of any information held about you on the register. Small fees are payable both for registration and to get copies of information from a data holder.

Remember also that any of your customers or staff might demand information about themselves. If you keep staff references or confidential comments on customers on computer, you must be prepared to show it to them if asked. If you do not wish to do that, keep the information out of your computer's memory.

Only you will know when the business is ready to expand. Well, no - you may be too near to it to see the obvious. The detached observer may be the best judge of this. Yet again, this is something on which to get the experts in. Don't forget you can go back to your local enterprise agency for help here either generally or to discuss what sort of expertise to tap. Your accountants, bankers and lawyers may also have a role to play. The DTI's Enterprise Initiative is aimed at encouraging small businesses to seek expert advice - and will pay part of the bill.

Plans to expand involve reassessing the things looked at already in this book, but from a stronger base. Questions of location need reviewing, as will the business structure. If it is getting beyond one person, it needs to become at least a partnership or probably a company. It will also need recapitalising.

Whilst there are many ways to expand, it is less risky to expand from strength. Your strength lies in your existing products and your existing customers. The safe routes forward are to sell your present products to new customers or to sell new products to your existing customers. Of course, the bigger the product range and the larger your customer bank, the wider your range of options. But if you try selling a new product to a new customer, you are in uncharted waters. Even the biggest companies can lose their way doing this - smaller businesses can seldom afford the risk.

EXPAND FROM STRENGTH

Another route forward is to buy someone else's product range and customers by acquiring or merging with another business. Aggressive expansion of businesses usually takes place through this route. It may be to increase the national spread of a business, or to buy out a rival, or to diversify into a compatible area of business. This is often called 'horizontal' expansion. You can also aim to integrate your business 'vertically' that is, link all the stages of business from first production to final sale to customer. Manufacturers do this when they open up their own stores. Steps of this sort involve considerable cash allocations, and require expert advice. For example, the major firms of accountants maintain a shared data bank of businesses for sale; if you are looking for a business, they can help in several ways.

EXPANDING OVERSEAS

We are now a few years into our membership of the Single Internal Market, and of the European Economic Area. This means you can export goods and services without customs duties or other major restrictions to any of the following states: Austria, Belgium, Denmark, Finland, France, Germany, Greece, Iceland, Ireland, Italy, Luxembourg, Netherlands, Norway, Portugal, Spain, and Sweden. You will find no barriers to exporting goods or services to any of these states, providing they comply with any special safety regulations, and with the general requirements of European law. There is now no legal difference in selling there to selling here. However, some points such as taxation do have to be watched because, of course, they are different in those countries. Equally they can sell goods and services in the UK. And they do.

Should you be looking overseas for part of your market?

Raising money the second time around may prove easier than at the start, if the business shows it knows what it is up to. It has the advantage of being able to produce accounts and balance sheets to show what has happened, and of being able to get capital from a wider range of sources for both long-term and short-term funding.

If its plans are big enough, it will have access to the **venture capital** market of long-term funding. This offers a wide range of finance available either as loans, or for buying a share of the **equity** of the business. That is, the financier will become part-owner by buying part of the company's share capital. This is a highly specialist field, and needs approaching through an adviser such as a banker or one of the major accountants with access to the necessary contacts, but the **British Venture Capital Association** (address at end) will give more details.

Other possibilities for short-term finance open up, as the company is a surer prospect. It can sell its debts. This is done by **factoring,** the process of getting a factor to collect your debts for you. The factor will advance you much of the money covered by the debts (perhaps 80 per cent), at interest, and then collect the debts and account to you for the balance, less charges. Contact the **Association of British Factors** (address at end) to find out more.

Another method of freeing company cash resources is by **leasing** equipment rather than buying it. This involves the company arranging for a finance house to buy capital items on behalf of the business, and then renting the assets to the business. The company ties up no capital assets, but has instead a predictable revenue and (tax-deductible) expenditure over the useful life of the asset. The **Equipment Leasing Association** will provide further information (address at end).

Banks will remain major lenders to larger businesses, not least because they have their own venture capital branches. If your bankers have followed you loyally so far, they are not likely to desert you now! But there are many alternatives, and all should be investigated as indicated.

Addresses

Accepting Houses Committee
Granite House
101 Cannon St
London EC4N 5BA

Institute of Chartered Accountants in England and Wales
Chartered Accountants Hall
PO Box 433
Moorgate Place
London EC2P 2BJ

Institute of Chartered Accountants of Scotland
27 Queen St
Edinburgh EH2 1LA

Chartered Association of Certified Accountants
29 Lincolns Inn Fields
London WC2A 3EE

Institute of Practitioners in Advertising
44 Belgrave Square
London SW1X 8QS

Advertising Standards Authority
Brook House
2-16 Torrington Place
London WC1E 7HN

Business in the Community
8 Stratton St
London W1X 5FD

Scottish Business in the Community
Eagle Star House
25 St Andrews Square
Edinburgh EH2 1AF

Association of British Chamber of Commerce
4 Westwood House
Westwood Business Park
Coventry CV4 8HS

Companies Registration Office
ENGLAND AND WALES
Companies House
Crown Way
Maindy
Cardiff CF4 3UZ
N. IRELAND
Dept. of Economic Development
64 Chichester St
Belfast BT1 4JX
SCOTLAND
102 George St
Edinburgh EH2 4DJ

National Cooperative Development Agency
Broadmead House
21 Panton St
London SW1Y 4DR

and

Holyoake House
Hanover St
Manchester M60 OAS

Data Protection Registry
Springfield House
Water Lane
Wilmslow
Cheshire SK9 5AX

Design Council
28 Haymarket
London SW1Y 4SU

Rural Development Commission
141 Castle St
Salisbury
Wiltshire SP1 3TP

Welsh Development Agency
Pearl House
Greyfriars Rd
Cardiff CF1 3XX

Disabled Living Foundation
380 Harrow Road
London W9 2HU

DTI (Dept of Trade and Industry)
HQ telephone : 071 215 5000
Enterprise Initiative freephone :
0800 500 200

**DTI Export Market Information
Centre**
Ashdown House
123 Victoria St
London SW1E 6RB

DTI Business in Europe Branch
66-74 Victoria St
London SW1E 6SW

Regional contacts for
Consultancy Initiative:

Birmingham:
77 Paradise Circus
Queensway
B2 2DT
Bristol:
The Pithay
BS1 2PD
Cambridge:
The Westbrook Centre
Milton Rd
CB4 1YG
Leeds:
25 Queen St
LS1 2TW
Liverpool:
Graeme House
Derby Square
L2 7UP
London:
Bridge Place
88-89 Eccleston Square
SW1V 1PT
Manchester:
Sunley Tower
Piccadilly Plaza
M1 4BA
Newcastle upon Tyne:
Stanegate House
2 Groat Market NE1 1YN
Nottingham:
Severns House
20 Middle Pavement
NG1 7DW

English Estates
St George's House
Kingsway
Team Valley
Gateshead NE11 ONA

Enterprise and Deregulation Unit
Dept. of Employment
Caxton House
Tothill St
London SW1H 9HF

Equal Opportunities Commission
Overseas House
Quay St
Manchester M3 3HN

European Commission
Information Centres
Telephone :
071 828 62 01 (London)
041 221 09 99 (Glasgow)
0222 22 95 25 (Cardiff)
0232 49 10 31 (Belfast)
to find your nearest office.

British Exporters Association
16 Dartmouth St
London SW1H 9BL

Association of British Factors
24-28 Bloomsbury Way
London WC1A 2PX

Office of Fair Trading
Field House
Breams Building
London EC4A

British Franchise Association
Thames View
Newtown Rd
Henley-on-Thames
Oxfordshire RG9 1HG

Highlands and Islands Enterprise
Bridge House
27 Bank St
Inverness IV1 1QR

Hotel and Catering Training Co
3 Denmark Street
London WC2H 8LP

ICOM (Industrial Common Ownership Movement)
Vassali House
20 Central Rd
Leeds LS1 6DE

Association of Independent Businesses
Trowbray House
108 Weston St
London SE1 3QF

Confederation of British Industry
Centre Point
103 New Oxford St
London WC1A 1DU

Industry Department for Scotland
Alhambra House
45 Waterloo St
Glasgow G2 6AT

Welsh Office Industry Department
Cathays Park
Cardiff CF1 3NQ

Central Office of Information
Hercules Rd
London SE1 7DU

Instant Muscle
84 North End Rd
London W14 9ES
(also regional offices)

**British Insurance Brokers
Association**
BIBA House
14 Bevis Marks
London EC3A 7NT

Association of British Insurers
51 Gresham St
London EC2VB 7HQ

**Ismaeli Business Information
Centre**
1 Cromwell Gardens
London SW7 2SL

The Law Society
113 Chancery Lane
London WC2A 1PL

Law Society of Scotland
26 Drumsheugh Gardens
Edinburgh EH13 7YR

Livewire
ENGLAND
Freepost, Newcastle upon Tyne
NE1 1BR
N. IRELAND
Freepost, Belfast BT7 1BR
SCOTLAND
Freepost,
Newton Mearns, Glasgow G77
5BR
WALES
Freepost, Cardiff CF1 1YT

British Institute of Management
Management House
Cottingham Rd
Corby
Northants NN17 1TT

**Institute of Management
Consultants**
32 Hatton Garden
London EC1

Institute of Marketing
Moor Hall
Cookham
Maidenhead
Berks SL6 9QH

Mid Wales Development
Ladywell House
Newtown
Powys SY16 IJB

**Northern Ireland Dept. of
Economic Development**
Aid to Industry Branch
22 Donegal St
Belfast BT1 2GP

**Northern Ireland Local
Enterprise Development Unit**
LEDU House
Upper Galwally
Belfast BT8 4TB

The Open University
PO Box 76
Milton Keynes MK7 6AN

British Overseas Trade Board
1 Victoria St
London SW1

Chartered Institute of Patent Agents
Staple Inn Buildings
High Holborn
London WC1V 7PZ

The Patent Office
Cardiff Rd
Newport
Gwent NP9 1RH

Institute of Patentees and Inventors
Suite 505A
Triumph House
189 Regent St
London W1R 7WF

Production Engineering Research Association
Nottingham Rd
Melton
Leics LE13 OPB

Project Fullemploy
102 Park Village East
London SW1 3SP

Institute of Purchasing and Supply
Easton House
Easton on the Hill
Stamford
Lincs PE9 3NZ

Scottish Development Agency
120 Bothwell St
Glasgow G2 7JP

Scottish Industry Department (IDS)
Sandyford Rd
Paisley
Glasgow G2 6AT

National Federation of Self-Employed and Small Businesses
32 St Annes Rd West
Lytham St Annes
Lancs FY8 1NY

Small Business Bureau
46 Westminster Palace Gardens
London SW1P 1RR

Small Firms Division, DTI
Steel House
Tothill St
London SW1H 9NF

British Standards Institution
2 Park St
London W1A 2BS

Business Statistics Office
Cardiff Rd
Newport
Gwent NP9 1XG

Institute of Taxation
12 Upper Belgrave Square
London W1

English Tourist Board
Thames Tower
Blacks Rd
London W6

Scottish Tourist Board
23 Ravelston Terrace
Edinburgh EH4 3EU

Welsh Tourist Board
Brunel House
2 Fitzalan Rd
Cardiff CF2 1U

Training and Enterprise Councils
Established locally throughout
the UK.
To find your nearest TEC
telephone
0800 300 787, or
0800 500 200
(Enterprise Initiative).

**British Venture Capital
Association**
3 Catherine Place
london SW1E 6DX

Welsh Development Agency
Pearl Building
Greyfriars Rd
Cardiff CF1

Women in Enterprise
26 Bond St
Wakefield
Yorks WF1 2QP

**The Prince's Youth Business
Trust**
5th Floor
5 Cleveland Place
London SW1Y 6JJ

Index